S0-BAK-878

Kick & Sandra

FATHERING A SON

From the Library

FATHERING A SON

By
PAUL HEIDEBRECHT
and
JERRY ROHRBACH

MOODY PRESS
CHICAGO

© 1979 by
THE MOODY BIBLE INSTITUTE
OF CHICAGO

All rights reserved

Library of Congress Cataloging in Publication Data

Heidebrecht, Paul.
   Fathering a son.

   Bibliography: p. 189.
   1. Boys. 2. Fathers and sons. 3. Children—Management.
I. Rohrbach, Jerry, joint author. II. Title.

HQ775.H44   649'.132   78-21871

ISBN 0-8024-3356-1

Printed in the United States of America

Contents

To Priscilla and Barbara,
our loving wives and partners
in the job of being fathers

Acknowledgments

This book represents two years of planning, dreaming, researching, and writing. Even more, it represents the grace of God, who gave us wonderful wives and children and the task of being husbands and fathers. This grace enabled us to start the job of being fathers and created the joy we have in writing about it. For this grace we are thankful, and before all who read this book, we acknowledge the goodness of the Lord.

We also acknowledge the ministry in which we are engaged. God has used Christian Service Brigade (CSB) for more than forty years to reach boys for Jesus Christ and to build Christian men. We are grateful that we have been privileged to serve in this ministry. Through our work, we have learned to know many Christian men, including some of the finest in our evangelical churches, and we have learned to know boys of all ages and sizes. We thank CSB for giving us a part in its ministry.

There are many individuals for us to thank. We are grateful to our executive director, Sam Gray, who spurred us on in this task, and to the fellow members of our program department at CSB, in particular Don Dixon, Rick Mould, and Woody Dahlberg, who put up with us and our shenanigans during those years. We thank our secretary, Mary Feldman, who helped us get this book written and to the publisher. To our friends at Moody Press, especially Les Stobbe, who were interested in our project from the start, we give our thanks. To the sisters at the Fellowship Deaconry in Elburn, Illinois, who hosted us for the final week of writing, we here offer our gratitude. And to a host of others—school teachers, mothers, Wheaton College students, fellow CSB staff members, and most of all, fathers who shared with us their victories and defeats— we give our thanks. It is for them that this book is written.

Foreword

In an age when the typical family is characterized by an "absent" father and a working mother, here is a welcome book. The title describes its contents—*Fathering a Son.*

As I read this manuscript for the first time, I was very pleasantly surprised. Frankly, I somewhat expected it to be filled with the ideals and perfectionist attitudes so common among young Christian fathers who are rearing their first sons. But not so! It is indeed a practical guide.

I was also impressed with the authors' caution in attempting to keep the reader's guilt level within bounds. How easy it is to create anxiety in the area of parental effectiveness! We have all failed and will continue to fail. The important thing is what we are doing to correct our errors. And this book will help us. It is both preventative and corrective.

As a father of three (one a son), I received help from this book. As a professor in the field of Christian education for a number of years, I was impressed with both its spiritual and its psychological insights. And, as a pastor, I recommend it to parents.

GENE A. GETZ

Introduction:
You Can Be a Good Father

You may remember the haunting, melodious "Cat's in the Cradle," a song by Harry Chapin, that was popular a few years ago. In the song, Chapin tells of a busy father's promises to his son that "We'll get together then; you know we'll have a good time then." Many years later, the grown son repeats the same words to his father, who then realizes that his boy has become just like him—too busy to spend time together.

The lyrics of that song stab deep into the hearts of thousands of fathers; fathers who, looking back over the years, wish they had spent more time with their sons; fathers who, peering ahead into the future, worry that they may make the same mistake and neglect their children.

This book is about being a father. You accepted the job of being a father when you married your wife and she gave birth to your child. The work of a father is also a vocation God gave you. He will hold you accountable, but He will also give you the resources to manage. Being a father is the one responsibility for which most fathers have the least preparation and about which they feel the most guilty.

This book is designed to put your mind at ease. We do not intend to make you feel guilty, but instead want to give you the help you need. You may need information about your son; we try to provide it in simple language. You may need guidelines in particular skills of parenthood, such as disciplining or teaching your son about sex; we provide those, too. Or you may need to be pushed, gently but firmly; we will try to motivate you to spend meaningful time with your son, not by haranguing or moralizing but by showing you the excitement of father-son relationships.

This book is written for the average father in the average Christian home in North America. Sure, we know that no "average father" exists, just as no "average son" exists. But there are thousands upon thousands of fathers who are not trained in child psychology and educational methodology. You have children whom you want to raise properly. You have learned from the mistakes of other fathers, but you see yourself making similar errors. You see yourself being submerged in the pressures of work, church, and community, and without realizing it, you may be losing touch with your son.

You will notice the light and easy format of this book. That is intentional, because there is another fact about "average fathers" that we recognize. They do not read very much. They do not buy many books, especially thick books about being good parents. This book is not meant to be read cover to cover. You can pick and choose according to what you need. Part 2 in particular (chaps. 7-13) is not meant to be read from chapter to chapter. Those chapters describe the developmental characteristics of your growing son from birth to age eighteen. You will be interested in the chapter dealing with your son's present age.

Who are we to be writing this book? We are both young fathers with young children. Our parental responsibilities have just begun. We believe that the task of being fathers is the most important job God has given us, but we do not think we have been given much help in doing that job.

We have read just about every book we could find on the subject of parenthood. Only a handful are written for fathers. We have talked to fathers, mothers, schoolteachers, and educators. We have worked hard to be knowledgeable so that we can write credibly. In the end, however, we write from our hearts, because that is where fatherhood begins. We are our own audience, yet we are deeply concerned about you. We all have to learn together to make the important task of fatherhood as fulfilling as God intended it to be.

Before we begin exploring the world of fatherhood, we want to point out several biases that we have. First, we will be dealing primarily with father-son relationships. This bias does not mean we lack concern for girls; much of what you will find in this book applies to your daughters as well as to your sons. One chapter deals with the unique features of the father-daughter relationship. But our concern at this moment is for your sons.

Sons become fathers and pattern their methods as fathers after the ways of their fathers. The need for starting positive, biblical patterns is obvious, and we hope this book will help.

Both of us work for an organization that is dedicated to helping local churches prepare their men to relate to boys. Our business is developing boys into Christian men who will be leaders in the church and community. We think the father-son relationship is the first and best way to do this.

We are not male chauvinists, and we have the greatest respect for Christian women who are seeking to be the women that God wants them to be. We hope our daughters will become truly liberated women who will serve Christ with all the gifts He gives them.

We are promasculine. We believe men—and the boys growing up behind them—need to be liberated. Too many false images of masculinity have been foisted upon us. One of those false images is that of the uninvolved, uninformed father. This false image has contributed to many societal ills, such as the breakdown of family unity, juvenile delinquency, the corruption of morals at all levels, and the spread of homosexuality, to name just a few. We believe that liberating men to be good

15

fathers to their sons would be an immense help in correcting these problems.

Second, we are Christians. Frankly, we do not know how we could be effective fathers without the help and direction of the Triune God—Father, Son, and Holy Spirit. God created us to be fathers, so it makes sense to follow His guidelines. Those guidelines, we believe, are found in the Bible.

Because we are Christians, we know we can be effective fathers. We can pray constantly to our Father who is in heaven and know that through His Spirit He will help us and our sons. When we make mistakes—and we will make many—we can receive forgiveness from God and therefore have the boldness to ask our sons to forgive us, too. Because we know that who we are is more important to our sons than what we say, we can rejoice that God's business is to redesign us to be like His Son, Jesus, the best model you can ever imagine. With a combination like that, it is hard to lose.

Third, we are convinced that you and we can be good fathers. That may be hard to believe when you read the statistics. Fathers are known for how little time they spend with their sons, not for how much they influence them. It does not have to be that way.

You have to decide that being a father to your son has higher priority than your vocation or hobbies. We hope this book will help you make that decision. Enjoy the book, talk about it with your wife, keep it for reference, and above all, put it down from time to time to be with your son.

PART 1

WELCOME TO THE JOB OF BEING A FATHER

"What do I do next?"

ONE

A Description of Your Job

Can you still remember the day your first child was born? After five years, Bill Jackson recalls the day vividly. He walked out of the hospital "in a daze. It was the first time I'd ever seen a baby born. I remember I felt funny saying the name 'Steven,' the name we picked for our son. There was a real person that belonged to that name!"

As Bill put the key into his car's ignition, his mind was overwhelmed: *Wow, I'm really a father now. I have a son. What am I supposed to do? Where do I start?* The thoughts were not exactly new. They had arisen many times during the previous nine months.

I'm not sure I'm ready for this, Bill kept thinking while his clammy hands gripped the steering wheel. *I'm not sure I know how to be a good father. Well, I guess Dad didn't know much more when I was born. You learn by trial and error, I suppose. Well, Lord, there's no turning back now, but I sure am going to need Your help.*

WHAT IS EXPECTED OF YOU

Somewhere in Bill's postdelivery musings, possibly you can see yourself. Amid all the thrills of becoming a father, you probably could not help wondering what a father does when he raises a son.

As in any occupation, a job description can be very helpful. Unfortunately, a job description for fatherhood is not provided by your doctor or the hospital. Nor will you find it in many books on parenthood. Here is our attempt to provide a simple but comprehensive overview of your job.

We have outlined six specific areas in which you should help your son develop all through his growing-up years. You can count them on your fingers: (1) independence; (2) security; (3) self-discipline; (4) spiritual growth; (5) sexual understanding; and (6) preparation for adult living.

We will describe each of these tasks briefly so that you can understand what is expected of you. Each will be explored in greater depth in later chapters of the book. Be sure to take advantage of the Personal Evaluator on page 28 to think through this job description.

INDEPENDENCE

Independence is that natural urge in all of us to act on our own, to be our own person, to express our individuality. As a father, you will see this independence emerge in your son in his first few months of life, grow all through his boyhood years, explode when he is a teenager, and finally settle in mature adulthood. The marks of an independent son are:

- an ability to take care of himself
- an honest recognition of his own strengths and weaknesses
- a sense of responsibility for himself and other people
- a desire to explore the world around him
- a courage to stand on his own, apart from everyone else.

You cannot make your son independent. You have to allow him to grow naturally, the way God made him. The most important task you have is to give him the right opportunities at the right time that will increase his independence. There is no easy formula for doing this. With the help of your wife, you have to learn what your son can handle.

It is very easy to overstep in either direction. You can push your son too hard, trying to make him too independent too

20

soon. For example, a father may give his two-year-old son a two-wheeler when a tricycle will do; he may send his seven year old to camp when he has never been away from home before; or he may make his teenage son work long hours at a job. A boy will get frustrated if too much is expected of him. He may not feel free to confide in his father and admit his mistakes or fears. He may then create a shell around himself—a "tough guy" image—while inside he will be hungering for a dependent relationship.

On the other hand, you can be overprotective and shelter your son from challenges or tasks that will teach him responsibility. A boy can become overly dependent on his parents, afraid to try new adventures for fear of making mistakes, perhaps lazy and unwilling to take responsibility, and hesitant to be open with others.

Why are you as a father so important? At least two reasons can be given. First, you are probably concerned about independence because it is a key to success in your own occupation. No doubt you place a high premium on being your own man. Your son will see this because you are the bridge to the outside world for him. Your example of independence is a huge factor in itself. Second, you need to balance your wife's influence. She may be overprotective, wanting to shelter your son from any potential harm. You can make it your job to challenge and test him. Or she may be the pushy one who will let your son try anything, so you may have to play the role of the protector. Working as a well-balanced team, you and your wife can direct your son toward independent growth.

SECURITY

Security is the atmosphere of freedom in which your son's independence can grow. A sense of security frees him from fear, doubt, and uncertainty and allows him to enjoy himself, his family, and the world around him.

Feeling secure in his family relationships will allow your

21

son to enter confidently into relationships with other people. He can handle rejection from others, such as a girlfriend, or a punch in the face by a neighborhood bully, when he can come back to you as a source of encouragement and love. At the same time, he can open himself to other people (such as his future wife) without fear, because he has learned to do it with you. A boy's lack of a sense of security can result in negative feelings about himself and other people that can contribute to all sorts of problems.

How can you give your son these feelings of security? Your physical contact with him is the place to start. When he is an infant, hold him often. Show affection frequently. Comfort him when he is hurt. As he gets older, an arm around the shoulder or a tussle of his hair has the same effect.

Then show this affirmation verbally. Tell him that you love him, no matter what his age. Congratulate him when he does well in anything. Work hard to avoid negative criticism and sarcasm. Let him know that you think he is valuable to you, even when he fails or disobeys.

Why are you so important? Because you are physically stronger and have a larger build than your wife, you will make a significant impression upon your son, especially in his early years. You can protect him from harm, hold him when he is afraid, and playfully roughhouse with him. You stand between him and a world that often frightens him.

As your son grows older, he will realize that physical strength by itself is not sufficient to keep him safe. But then he will see you as a man who has learned to cope with problems and take initiative to find solutions. Of course, he will see your weaknesses, too. That is when your dependence on God can add to his sense of security and serve as a model for where his ultimate security should rest.

SELF-DISCIPLINE

Self-discipline in your boy is one of the most satisfying fruits of many years of raising a son. A father has served his son well when he has given him the ability to live a responsible, aggressive, and obedient life under the control of his own will. A self-disciplined boy will be able to meet challenges, solve problems, and constantly improve his own knowledge and abilities.

On the road to self-discipline, you have several important tasks to perform. First, you have to correct your son's behavior, especially in the early, formative years of his life. Second, you have to teach him to solve problems on his own. Third, you must instill in him a motivation to achieve goals that he sets for himself or that are set for him by others.

When you correct your son's behavior, you do several things for him. You help him understand the concept of authority. Every person needs to understand, respect, and obey authority, whether it is the authority of parents, the law, or God. Otherwise, life becomes miserable. You acquaint him with the "rules of the road," or basic guidelines, for getting along with other people. They give him limits in which he can live with a sense of security. You also establish patterns of positive behavior that he will follow for the rest of his life. Simply punishing him for a misdeed does not accomplish this. You need to explain how he should act, and then encourage him to move in that direction.

You can give your son problem-solving ability by simply challenging him at every step in his life. In infancy, the challenge may be to find a ball under a blanket. In boyhood, he can decide what he will do with the money he has earned cutting grass. In his teen years, you can let him make his summer plans or select a college or trade school. Give yourself the job of setting hurdles before your son that will force him to use his mind. Do not let him get frustrated so that he quits, but let him work out problems on his own.

You can also be a powerful example of a problem solver when, for example, you try to repair the lawnmower or complete your income tax returns. To help your son, you have to involve him in the problem-solving process, giving him certain tasks to do that help you, or simply listening to his advice. As soon as he is able, he should participate in the making of major family decisions.

The desire to achieve goals and enjoy useful, productive activities can make the big difference between a satisfying life and an aimless, unproductive one. Early in his life, your son needs to be shown by you how to set a goal (e.g., save a dollar to buy a toy) and work toward it. School and church will impose many new goals. Your encouragement in those areas will be crucial. Your personal example is the biggest factor in motivating your son to achieve. If you set goals for your own life and work toward them, you will influence him far more than any lectures on doing well. You must be careful to balance an emphasis on achievement with an emphasis on healthy relationships with people. It will do your son little good to have a successful career if he abuses people in order to succeed.

SPIRITUAL GROWTH

In various passages of the Bible, you will find specific directions for fathers. We believe they are from God, because the Bible is His communication to mankind. God places upon fathers the responsibility for the spiritual welfare of their families. Mothers have an equally influential role, but the task of spiritual leadership has been given to fathers. In chapter 3 we will explore Scripture to discover what it teaches about fatherhood.

For now, let's clarify what you need to do for your son's spiritual growth. As with independence, you cannot force spiritual growth in your son. Spiritual growth is the work of God's Holy Spirit. What you can do is provide the best possible conditions for your son to learn and experience the new life received from Christ.

How do you do this?

24

• Live up to your position as an authority figure. Your son's understanding of God is greatly influenced by his relationship to you. Your firm leadership and discipline of his life will help him understand what kind of person God is.

• Be an example of a praying, Bible-reading, people-loving Christian. Let your faith be obvious so that your boy can see an honest Christian. Even if you do not think you are a good example of a Christian, do not hide your shortcomings. When you fail, admit it. Honesty and humility are the marks of a Christian, anyway.

• Teach your son the truths and principles of God's Word. Better yet, learn them together with him. Consider yourself the number one instructor, not the Sunday school. Tell him Bible stories when he is young, and study the teachings of Jesus and Paul when he is older.

• Pray for him constantly. Pray that he will accept Christ when he is old enough to understand. Pray that he will live out the Christian life as a child, teen, and adult.

• Share experiences and talk with him. Discuss spiritual truths as soon as he can talk. Use everyday conversations for spiritual discussions—do not wait for specifically devotional times.

SEXUAL UNDERSTANDING

Your son's sexual understanding will develop from many sources, but you are one of the most important. How he will relate to girls as a teenager, adjust to sexual union with his future wife, and what he will think about his own body are all dependent on what you teach and show him by example. You give him sex education no matter what you do or do not do. You have several responsibilities if you want to do your job right.

• Give him the facts as he is able to understand them. When he begins to ask questions about the human body or about

25

babies, answer him in simple, accurate language. Lead family conversations about the purpose of sex. Point out the sexual misconceptions and misconduct that your son might watch on television, see on billboards, or hear from playmates. Aim to give your son the "straight scoop" first rather than leaving him to figure things out for himself with the wrong information that other children give him.

● Establish an atmosphere of freedom in your home to talk about any matter related to sex. Shock, mockery, and embarrassment should have no place there. Be frank, honest, and open.

● Show by example your prior commitment to your wife. Let your son know clearly that his mother is the most important person to you. Spend time with her away from the children. Do not be afraid to be affectionate toward her when your son is around. When he disobeys or treats her disrespectfully, let him know quickly that you will not tolerate it.

● Respect your son's physical accomplishments. Even if he is not an athlete, communicate a respect for him and his body. Remember, the human body is God's creation and temple. Thank God for your own body, and encourage your son to thank God for his body.

PREPARATION FOR ADULT LIVING

The acid test of all your fatherly work will come when your son steps into the adult world, obtains a job or continues his education, marries and starts his own family, or simply leaves your home to live his own life. As you look forward to that day, several concerns should occupy your mind. Those concerns may prompt you to some action now.

Can he get along with other people? Relationships with all kinds of people characterize the adult world. Your son needs to be in the preparation stage now. Expose him to many of your friends and neighbors. Let him meet strangers. Show him by example how to get acquainted and maintain a conversation. Teach him how to react to people who mistreat or cheat him. Encourage him to be fair and honest. Help him to ask for forgiveness when he has wronged someone.

Will his school education help him with his future career? Keep a practical emphasis in mind as you observe your son's progress through school. Take an active interest in what he is learning, and help him explore all future career possibilities. Get involved with his school to be sure your son is getting the most profitable education possible.

Will he be a good husband and father? Your example is obviously the major factor in determining the answer because in many ways, he will be just like you. Give him fatherly responsibilities as he is able to handle them, such as babysitting. When he begins to date, talk to him about husband-wife relationships from your own experience.

Will he be a leader in the church and community? Give yourself the privilege of helping your son into the "real world" of leadership and responsibility. Encourage him to show concern for those in need and take leadership when the opportunity is in front of him.

Personal Evaluator

Job descriptions are not meant only to tell you what you must do; they are also useful for evaluating how well you are doing once you have started working. Try answering the questions in the Personal Evaluator that follows, both now and after you have read the book.

PERSONAL EVALUATOR

Your Responsibility	Ask Yourself	Discuss with Your Wife
1. Independence	1. How would I grade my son in independence? What is my long-range goal for my son's independent growth?	1. Is our son as independent for his age as he could be? Do we give him the freedom to make mistakes? How do we balance each other in challenging our son's independence?
2. Sense of Security	2. How secure do I feel with God? Do I feel free to be affectionate and tender with my son?	2. How does our son feel about himself and the world around him? How well does he interact with children and adults? Do we encourage him more than we criticize him?
3. Self-discipline	3. Am I correcting my son's behavior or just punishing him out of anger? Do I set goals for my life and then work toward them?	3. What is our ultimate goal in the disciplining of our son? Do we work together as a team? How do we involve our son in problem solving?
4. Spiritual Growth	4. Am I growing spiritually? Can I talk about it with my family? Am I assuming the spiritual leadership of my home?	4. Is our home a good environment for spiritual growth? How much biblical instruction are we giving to our son? Do we discuss spiritual truths in daily conversations?
5. Sexual Understanding	5. How do I treat my wife in front of my son? How do I respond to my son's physical accomplishments, or lack of them?	5. Do we have an atmosphere of freedom in our home to discuss sex? Is our son getting accurate information about sex? Are we showing him by example how wonderful marriage can be?
6. Preparation for Adult Living	6. How concerned am I about my son's education? Am I concerned about setting a good example as a husband and father?	6. How does our son get along with other children? Does he interact comfortably with adults other than ourselves? Are we giving him training for fatherhood now?

28

TWO

You Make All the Difference

You are a father for a purpose. You have a central place in your family. Your children need you.

When God designed the family, He built into it certain functions for the father. Discovering what those functions are can be thrilling for any father who wonders what contribution he is making to his family. Sociologists and psychologists have discovered numerous effects of fatherly involvement and fatherly absence. What they have discovered serves to confirm the importance God placed upon the father.

Much of what follows can be applied to your wife. She is your partner in each of your family functions. But your leadership is the key to success, and your failure can result in great difficulties.

WHY YOU ARE IMPORTANT

POSITIVE SELF-IMAGE

The way you treat your child determines how he will feel about himself. Your opinion of him will become his opinion of himself.

As the father, you can give your child the gift of high self-esteem. You can help him have a healthy appreciation for himself, a self-confidence that helps him cope with success and failure.

"Great picture, son."

30

If you respect him, trust him, show interest in him, and compliment him, you increase his sense of self-worth. Sarcasm, verbal abuse, and simply not spending time with him destroy his self-esteem and help prepare him for failure.

CONCEPT OF GOD

Theological understanding begins in a child's earliest years. He picks up impressions from experiences in the home and starts to organize his thoughts about God, Jesus, heaven, and himself. Of special importance is his image of you. In a sense, you represent God to him. If you are warm and affectionate to him, it is easy for him to feel attracted to God and to understand that God loves him. Your punishment of disobedience helps to show God's righteousness. On the other hand, a cold, harsh relationship with your child will often result in a distant, fearful attitude toward God.

UNDERSTANDING OF SEX ROLE

Your son's understanding of being a man and your daughter's understanding of being a woman depend in large measure upon you. Your relationship to your son and daughter is especially important. So is the way you treat your wife. We will say more about this in chapters 4 and 15.

MORAL VALUES AND ATTITUDE TOWARD AUTHORITY

In your family, you represent the values, standards, and regulations of the world in which your child lives. He sees you making decisions, reacting to authorities, and obeying the laws. Your submission to authority (e.g., God's Word) makes a big difference, just as does your personal commitment to moral and spiritual values (e.g., honesty).

LINK TO SOCIETY

One theory of fatherhood says that the father is the more important parent from a social standpoint: you are the one concerned about getting your son out into the world and learning to take care of himself. You prepare your son for his future career. You introduce him to the world outside the home. He learns from you how to relate to all kinds of people: neighbors, church members, relatives, and strangers.

Your wife has an important part in this socializing function as well. But your son tends to look to you for cues on how to get along outside the home. You provide a "second opinion on life" that balances the influences of the mother.

DESIRE TO ACHIEVE

A child's success in school and later in a career can be traced to a father's involvement. How? Your attitude about your own success or failure in an activity is passed on to your child. And your encouragement and support of his efforts stimulate him to work toward a goal. We will say more about this in chapter 17.

EFFECTS OF FATHER ABSENCE

Now let's look at the influence of the father from the other side. What happens when the father is not present in the family? This is the case in more than 10 percent of homes in the United States. A father can be absent from the home because of death, divorce, separation, or desertion. He can also be absent for long periods of time because his occupation requires it. The earlier this absence occurs in the child's life and the longer the absence, the more impact it has.

DELINQUENCY

A definite link has been found between juvenile delinquency and the absence of fathers from the home. There are numerous possible reasons for the link between the two. A boy may be resentful that his father has not cared for him. Likely he has not learned the self-control or respect for authority that a father can provide.

Boys with absent fathers tend to be more dependent on others and less aggressive. They do not have a positive view of themselves as males. What is lacking is the warm, affectionate father-son relationship. When a dominant or overaffectionate mother is added to this situation, a boy will have great difficulty understanding his own male identity. Although this is not the only reason for homosexuality, many homosexual males have dominant mothers and weak or absent fathers.

LOW ACHIEVEMENT

Boys without fathers show low scores in almost all areas of academic achievement, including mathematical, verbal, analytical and mechanical skills. Much of this relates to a boy's difficulty in adjusting to life without his father.

Henry Biller, a leading authority on the effects of parental absence, has indicated that it may be better for the children if the father is dead rather than divorced from the mother or otherwise separated from the family. The effect on the children is usually not as bad.

It should also be noted that as bad as father absence is, it is nonetheless better for the father to be absent than for him to be home and not involved with his child. Paternal neglect is actually more damaging than paternal absence; one reason for this is that children will look for father substitutes if they have no access to their own fathers.

A WORD FOR THE WEARY

In case you are feeling depressed about this chapter because you have not been a perfect father, relax. This is not a list of dos and don'ts that you must follow diligently to avoid failing miserably as a father. Rather, it is a description of how important you are to your son. If there is something to be learned from this chapter, it is this: take your job of being a father seriously. You are making an impact on the life of your son.

"Son, this is our guide to success."

THREE

What Our Father Thinks

The journey of fatherhood is long. God's promise that He will be with us always is refreshingly relevant. His Word provides guideposts for the journey. They are worth knowing and enjoying. They express what our Father's mind is for all fathers.

Becoming a father is a spiritual event for the Christian man. He recognizes that fatherhood is a calling. It is a God-given vocation, not unlike being a missionary, preacher, or teacher. To be a father is to play a major role in God's plan for His people, particularly in the teaching and training of children in the way of the Lord (Deuteronomy 6:4-9). The Old Testament shows how God uses parents, especially fathers, to transmit the values and truths of His Word to the following generation (Psalm 78:1-8; Isaiah 38:19). In the New Testament, the father is given responsibility for the spiritual nurture of his family (Ephesians 6:4).

The effective father recognizes that fatherhood is a mandate from God, and he accepts the responsibilities and privileges it brings. He makes a major investment of his time and energy in this calling. He knows there will be enjoyable and difficult times, but he knows also that the God who called him to this unique ministry will sustain him through it.

In his book *The Effective Father,* Gordon MacDonald uses the analogy of an orchestra conductor to describe the father's

35

pacesetting role. In the analogy, the father is the conductor, his family is the orchestra, and God is the composer of the music. The father's task is to make sure the "orchestra" plays the music the way the "composer" wrote it. In other words, his job is to make sure the members of his family are living the way God intends them to live.

How does the effective father set this kind of pace?

● By expecting obedience from his children and following through to make sure he gets it.

● By protecting his children from harmful influences and supervising their character development.

● By developing good habits in his children's lives.

● By dealing directly with sinful or immature behavior.

● By teaching God's standards for living, as found in the Bible (Deuteronomy 11:18-19).

● By living before his children the kind of life he wants them to live (Joshua 24:14-15).

All this develops a pace of life that his children can learn to follow.

God also expects fathers to be men who correct wrong behavior decisively. Because God is a just and holy God who hates sin, disobedience is taken very seriously by the effective father. He recognizes God's displeasure with sinful behavior and the painful consequences that follow (Proverbs 22:15). Therefore, he confronts his children with their wrong behavior and administers appropriate discipline as a consequence of misbehavior. He does not try to avoid these disciplinary situations, but acts promptly (Proverbs 6:23; 13:24). As a representative of God's righteousness, he makes sure his children recognize the seriousness of disobedience.

At the same time, the Christian father knows that God is a merciful, loving Father who provides forgiveness when a sinner repents and claims Christ's sacrifice on his behalf. Therefore, he follows his disciplining of his children with forgiveness and reconciliation. The misdeed is then forgiven and forgotten (Psalm 103:12-13).

God's kind of father teaches his children wisdom (Proverbs 4:1-13). Every father wants his children to have common sense and a practical knowledge of how to get along in the world. But the goal of the effective father is greater than that. He is concerned that his children look at life from God's perspective and act according to what is right in God's eyes. This is the kind of wisdom the Bible talks about. It is the same thing as being Christlike, or having the fruit of the Spirit. The effective father takes on the role of a teacher who instructs his children in the ways of wisdom. How does he do this?

First, the effective father sets an example of wise living (Proverbs 1:8-9). He deliberately lives according to the principles of God's Word in all situations, even when those principles are unpopular or his adherence to them results in some kind of hardship. He exhibits the fruit of the Spirit in his home. He seeks to be more Christlike in his character and actions, asking for help from his family and praying daily for God to produce Christ's qualities in him.

Second, he instructs his children in wisdom. He can do this in formal situations, such as family devotions, and in informal situations, such as when his son has a fight with a neighborhood friend. He carefully explains God's way of dealing with a situation and encourages the boy to act that way. The Bible is always this teacher's textbook.

Third, the effective father trains his children to act wisely (Proverbs 10:1; 29:3). During the formative years of his child's life, a father can help the child develop right ways of acting and wise ways of handling situations. Then, as the child grows, those patterns will be followed with regularity.

The Christian father builds self-discipline into his children's lives (Hebrews 12:5-11). This habit is based on the pattern of God's disciplining of us (Proverbs 3:11-12). One goal of a father's discipline of his children is to help them become self-disciplined. His close supervision of their behavior during their early years builds his confidence that they will act correctly even when he is not present. His aim is to instill in them the ability to control themselves; to do what is right in spite of pressure from others; to live obediently by their wills, not by feelings.

Building self-discipline means introducing stress into an older child's life. The effective father does this deliberately. He does not pamper his children or give them everything they want. Instead, he gives them experiences of working hard to earn something, learning to live with less, or simply doing without. Although he is always protective, he does not shield his older children from all hard experiences. Sometimes, he lets them fail or allows them to encounter a hostile environment if he sees some benefit in it for them.

Finally, a father must depend upon God to be effective. Gordon MacDonald talks about the effective father living on the edge of ineffectiveness. This man recognizes that he can easily fail or find himself in a situation in which he does not know what to do. Or his children can turn against him and reject the values and standards that he has diligently taught them. In those moments of despair and misery, the effective Christian father reaches out to his heavenly Father, who can lovingly and sovereignly work together for good all things, even a breakdown in the family's life.

Why does the effective father depend upon God? First, because all "success" as a father is a gift from God (1 John 2: 13-14). The positive response and spiritual growth of children manifest the work of the Spirit in their lives. Not that this father does not get any credit (or blame) for what he does, but he knows that the changes of heart and attitude that occur in his children are not his doing.

Second, no father is free from the possibility of failure, no matter how hard he tries (Deuteronomy 24:16). Children have their own wills and can choose to live in a manner different from what their parents wish. They can reject their parents and even God. The effective father is humbled by this knowledge and prays daily for his children. And like the father of the prodigal son, fathers can experience the joy of seeing their children return home.

Third, even though a father does fail, he knows that God accepts him and loves him. He knows that broken relationships can be restored by the power of God, and he puts his trust in that power. He admits his failure honestly to his children and works hard to improve.

Last, this father is aware of God's people in his church, community, and around the world who can influence his children positively. God uses other adults to build a father's children. For this the father is grateful. When he can no longer exert an influence on his children, he knows that other believers can.

"After this you can learn to change baby's diaper."

FOUR

Help Your Son Become a Man

We men are involved in a struggle of great significance to our families. The struggle is over our role as men in North American society. Each of us encounters that battle on several fronts, some obvious, others more subtle. How we engage in those skirmishes will determine how we feel about our own lives and what our sons will do with their lives.

When we talk about roles, male or female, we are talking about behavior that is expected of a person in society. There are certain ways in which men and women are expected to act.

Another way to describe these roles is with the concepts of *masculinity* and *femininity*. Both of these terms suggest certain attitudes, feelings, goals, and methods of relating to others that society expects will characterize a man considered "masculine" or a woman considered "feminine." When a man exhibits the expected "masculine" characteristics or a woman the expected "feminine" characteristics, he or she usually feels comfortable and accepted by others.

Unfortunately, male and female roles are not set in concrete. They change. What is expected of a man in one generation may not be required in the next, and likewise with women.

One reason for our present struggle is that the roles of men and women in North American society are undergoing a drastic change.

The women's liberation movement is probably the most significant factor in the changing of roles. It has won major victories over the bastions of so-called male supremacy. It has allowed women to carve out for themselves new responsibilities and new definitions of their role in society. And it has forced us to treat women as equal persons rather than as a second-class race.

The evangelical church is also experiencing the impact of this movement. Regardless of your own position on the ordination of women, you will discover that women are assuming areas of responsibility in the church usually delegated to the men.

Because of this new confidence that many women enjoy, we men are suddenly on the defensive. We can no longer assume certain facts about our role. More than half of the households in America have working mothers, so who is the breadwinner? We were once known as strong, independent, and success oriented; now more women are, too. As women invade each domain that we men have dominated, the questions begin to haunt us: What is left for us? What is unique about our role? What is genuinely masculine?

Many men have responded to this predicament in a healthy way. They have willingly accepted new sex-role boundaries and learned tasks normally done by women. They have spear-headed men's liberation groups, attempting to redefine their roles.

Others have reacted differently. Some have become bitter and antagonistic. Some have remained uninvolved, maintaining a low level of interest in reexamining their own role.

Those uninvolved men represent a second dimension to the struggle. They have for all practical purposes abdicated their responsibilities as husbands and fathers. They reinforce the image, often presented on television and generally accepted by the public, of a bungling, uncommunicative, and uninvolved father who prefers to go drinking with his buddies rather than take care of his children. Of course, many fathers are not like that. But these men must resist the norm of North American society, which is to ignore the importance of the father in child rearing. Fatherhood is not normally considered one of the highlights of being a man.

A complicating factor for some men in this struggle is their commitment to Jesus Christ and the authority of the Bible. These men are Christians, and they must resolve the many conflicts between the kind of life-style the Bible advocates and the kind of life-style that is traditionally considered masculine.

An added dimension comes from another heavily debated issue in North American society: homosexuality. In this case, a certain percentage of the population is attempting to redefine the masculine role to allow two men (or women) to form a family unit. A "gay" life-style introduces a whole new set of values with which all men will have to cope. The devastating effects of this movement are only beginning to be felt.

This sketchy description probably raises more questions than it answers. Certainly, it brings into focus the work that lies ahead for men, particularly Christian men, in attempting to understand what it takes to be a *real* man.

JESUS' KIND OF MAN

As young fathers, we have several responses to this challenge to traditional male-female roles:

First, we are grateful for many of the results of the women's liberation movement. Many of the stereotyped images of men (e.g., those epitomized by John Wayne, Archie Bunker, and the Marlboro man) were phony and needed to be destroyed. The unfair treatment of women (especially in employment practices) needed to be rectified. We are delighted that the issue of masculinity has come into the spotlight. We believe that the biblical revelation has much insight to offer on this subject.

Second, we recognize that priority must be placed on relating to each other as persons rather than as men and women. The Bible does not give a list of Christian masculine character-

43

istics; it shows what we must all be like. United in Christ, the distinctions between male and female break down (Galatians 3:28).

Yes, there are biological differences between men and women that result in personal, psychological differences (e.g., a woman's menstruation and consequent moody feeling, and a man's larger physical frame and ability to be protective). But neither sex has a corner on any particular personality trait. Most expectations of men and women are essentially cultural and are subject to change.

Third, because we see few significant differences between men and women beyond biologically related distinctions, we prefer to distinguish between Christian and non-Christian masculinity. At this point, a clear outline of masculinity for the Christian can be formulated.

Jesus is the example we use to develop this view. In Jesus, we see many characteristics that stand apart from those our society expects of a man. He cried openly on several occasions of which we are aware. He played with children and said that we must become like them in their simple faith. He treated women with respect and interacted with them on an intellectual level.

Other expectations emerge from the Bible for the Christian man. His qualities should include patience, kindness, gentleness, self-control, and faithfulness. God the Holy Spirit produces these in him (Galatians 5:22-23). He should be honest about himself and confess his failures (Romans 12:3; 1 John 1:9). Being an effective husband and father is also discussed in many passages. All these indicate that the Christian man is a spiritually alive and growing person.

But cannot all this be said of the Christian woman? Yes, the fruit of the Spirit, honesty, and confession should also characterize the Christian woman. This may suggest the major difference in the roles of Christian men and women. God has given men a leadership responsibility. What is this leadership

44

like? Jesus described it in Matthew 20:26. It is a servant-style leadership. This kind of leadership places emphasis on meeting the needs of the other person and helping that person to grow and mature. The Christian man's role involves this kind of leadership in the home. In succeeding chapters of this book, we will consider how to practice this kind of leadership.

WHERE DOES YOUR SON FIT IN?

Your son is an active participant in this struggle, too. From his earliest years, he engages in a process of identification with you. You are a model that he observes as he attempts to develop his concept of sex roles. He synthesizes his observations of you and the things he learns from school and neighborhood friends into his conception of the masculine role. The influence of your wife on him is another factor in this development. As one writer says, sex-role development is a complicated process.

Since you are an important person in the development of your son's understanding of sex roles, what can you do that will be an effective influence?

• Build the personal relationship between you and your son. Author Leonard Benson says that this is the crucial determinant in your son's masculinity. It is more important than any of the activities you do together. A relationship with your son is built on respect and acceptance of each other. It depends on your being honest with each other, confessing sins, and forgiving each other.

• Guard against having stereotyped expectations for your son. As much as possible, expect all your children to do every task around the house. Avoid delegating only certain things to boys. Make sure your son knows how to change a diaper, bake a cake, and sew on a button.

• Participate in child care starting from the day your child comes home from the hospital. The more you change diapers,

45

feed the baby, and watch him during illness, the more you provide a healthy, well-rounded image of a man.

• Exercise leadership in the home. Take the lead in spiritual instruction, discipline, training, and exposing your child to the world. Leadership and a close relationship make a powerful, positive combination in nurturing your son's masculine development.

FIVE

It's the Relationship that Counts

We have mentioned the importance of a personal relationship with your son several times. It is the secret to the positive influence you wish to have upon your son. And it is also the avenue by which God can use your son to help you grow. In this chapter we will discuss some of the essential elements in a father-son relationship.

BUILDING TRUST

Bill Adams was a brave man; at least that is what the other men of the fellowship said about him. He took many chances with his fifteen-year-old son, Tom. He let him take one of his credit cards on a weekend visit to Chicago. And he allowed him to set his own curfew on weekends.

But Bill was rarely disappointed in his son because he had built an atmosphere of trust with Tom. It started when Tom was still a small boy. Bill made a practice of expecting the best from his son, believing him at all times, and letting him know that he had great confidence in him. You could describe this as the 1 Corinthians 13 kind of love that "bears all things, believes all things, hopes all things, endures all things" (v. 7, NASB). Sure, Tom disobeyed and told lies, but Bill avoided the distrust, the constant checking up, and the nagging that he could have shown Tom. Instead, he looked for ways in which Tom could step out on his own, like riding the bus downtown by himself when he was eleven, and he supported him by con-

47

"How about the credit cards too, dad?"

stant encouragement. As Tom matured into his teen years, Bill began to treat him as a responsible young adult. He expressed his disappointment in Tom when Tom failed him, but he never gave up on the boy.

He assumed that Tom was trustworthy, and that is exactly what Tom became.

Trust is something that two people build. It is a quality in a relationship that allows each person to take risks with the other because he knows that the other will not let him down. Fathers can build trustworthiness in their sons by expecting trustworthy behavior of them; by being honest about their feelings toward them—when they behave or misbehave; by allowing their sons to be honest with them; by encouraging a free atmosphere in the home in which anyone can say what is on his mind without being attacked; and by giving their sons responsibilities and letting them fail and succeed in them.

ACTIVE LISTENING

Two years ago Bert Bannister made a startling discovery. He was driving to the grocery store. His son, Johnny, age six, was in the car with him. Johnny sat quietly, looking out the window. It suddenly occurred to Bert that Johnny seemed to reserve his usual chatter for his mother, whereas when he and Johnny were together, there was little conversation. Johnny had learned that his father was not interested in what he had to say. So he stopped talking.

When Bert realized his failure, he began to cultivate the habit of active listening. He encouraged Johnny to talk by asking him questions about the activities of the day. He probed each event with more questions and tried to get an accurate picture for himself of what life was like for Johnny. Bert listened for more than information; he listened for feelings, too, because they are very important.

Needless to say, Bert and Johnny grew much closer. Bert

realized that his times of active listening would pay rich dividends, both in the present and in the future.

Active listening is a special way to listen that helps build close relationships. It is more than hearing the words your son is saying to you. It is getting "inside his head" and then thinking along with his thoughts. It is working hard to fully understand what he is saying and how he is feeling. To do this, you must ask questions. Sometimes you must repeat back to your son what he has just told you to be sure that you have understood him. You must fight the temptation to dominate the conversation and instead simply let him talk, not endlessly or aimlessly, but in the direction of revealing himself to you.

SHOWING ACCEPTANCE

Phil Evans could not understand his son, Billy, for many years. For a ten year old, he seemed to show little interest in sports. He was shy, prone to crying, very sensitive, and easily hurt by harsh, cutting remarks. Phil had tried to be gentle toward Billy, but he knew he often failed.

Then Phil faced up to his own attitude toward Billy. He realized that he was not accepting Billy just as he was. He was rejecting him because Billy was not living up to Phil's preconceived image of a ten-year-old boy. So Phil decided to show some real acceptance.

Phil forced himself to be more affectionate. He showed interest in Billy's activities, complimented him on his efforts, and praised him to his mother. He told Billy frequently that he loved him very much and would accept him as his son no matter what Billy did with his life.

Slowly, Phil began to realize this kind of acceptance was no different from the kind God showed to him each day. He knew what that acceptance had done for him.

Showing acceptance means letting another person know that he is worthwhile, valuable, important, and loved. Every person needs to believe that he is accepted—by God through Jesus

50

Christ and by others who respect him for who he is. Showing acceptance to your son is indeed giving a great gift. Acceptance is shown verbally and nonverbally: verbally, by telling your son that you love him, by praising him for what he does, and by telling him that you appreciate him even when he fails or disobeys; nonverbally, by speaking kindly to him, by hugging and embracing him, and by giving him your full attention when he talks to you.

RESOLVING CONFLICTS

Reg Malinowsky and his teenage son, Marty, had their disagreements. Sometimes the music Marty listened to caused the disagreement. Other times it was Marty's study habits. Occasionally it was Reg's policies about the use of the family car.

But the disagreements did not pull this father and son apart. Instead, they were used in a constructive way to build the relationship.

Reg could always demand obedience, referring to Scripture if necessary. Marty would submit, but not happily. But Reg knew that he had to deal with his son as a growing adult and work out some of their differences as brothers in Christ.

So he—with Marty's help—developed a procedure for resolving conflicts. First, they would try to define the problem as simply as possible. They put it in writing, if necessary. Then each would state his feelings about the situation without attacking the other. Following that, they would list all the possible solutions they could imagine. Together they would select one and put it into practice for a week or two. Evaluation followed and changes were made. Both Reg and Marty found this to be a much more profitable and creative way to handle conflicts.

No relationships are without conflicts. The good relationships are those in which conflicts are handled constructively. Like all people, fathers and sons can learn some simple steps of conflict management that will lead to a closer relationship.

A conflict must be defined clearly. That requires the viewpoints of both parties. Possible solutions should be listed by both persons; one should be selected jointly, tried out, and evaluated. It helps to distinguish between your own feelings and reactions and your constant acceptance of the person with whom you disagree. Listening carefully to each other and even trying to state the other person's position are further steps to take.

COMMUNICATING

You could say that Merv Proctor had some problems communicating with his three teenagers. You could say that Merv had problems communicating with his wife, too, until they returned from a Christian marriage-enrichment seminar, at which they learned some techniques of communicating. Actually, what they learned was how to express their love in constructive, relationship-building ways. For the Proctors, love began to be communicated.

Merv decided to put some of the methods he had learned into action with his teens. His first task was to work toward a climate of open communication in the home. That meant avoiding unnecessary arguments and concentrating on praising his children for their strengths and accomplishments.

Rather than trying to force conversation with his teens, Merv relaxed and joined in their casual conversations. He learned more about them than he ever had before. When he told them his own feelings and ideas, Merv tried to be clear and honest without judging them. He told them that even if he did not like certain aspects of their activities or dress, he still loved them.

For Merv, communicating also meant not using unfair tactics, like bombarding his teens with criticisms, interrupting, jumping to conclusions, attacking their motives, letting his feelings get hurt easily, or becoming sarcastic.

The lack of communication is perhaps the number one

problem in most marriages today. It also may be the main problem in parent-teen relationships.

Communicating is not all that complicated; it is just hard work. It takes time, often time that you would rather spend doing something else.

How does a father begin communicating with his son? First, he must work on creating a nonjudgmental atmosphere. His love for his son is a key factor. This love must be unconditional, that is, with no strings attached. He loves his son no matter what the boy says or does. His actions and verbal promise prove this. This gives the son freedom to say what is on his mind or in his heart to his father, knowing he will not be condemned. Of course, a father may disagree strongly with his son, but he will not be shocked or offended.

Second, to communicate effectively a father should avoid the long lectures, a form of one-way communication. Like any other person, a boy can "tune out" while a man pours out his vast reservoir of knowledge. It is better to answer questions that a son asks and save the heavy instruction for the times when children are prepared for it.

Communication usually occurs best in informal settings (e.g., while driving a car or on a camping trip). Such settings are nonthreatening to teenagers, particularly, and can result in very honest discussion. Such occasions should be used for a great amount of listening. Ask questions and find out what a boy thinks and feels. Give him full attention. Look him in the eye, if possible.

Finally, a key to communication with a boy is to be ready to talk or listen when the boy wants to. A father who constantly tells his son that he is too busy (e.g., watching television or reading a newspaper) will eventually find that his son is too busy for him. Availability to a son, even if it is late at night, enhances a father's communication effectiveness. As one father said, "When a boy wants to talk, don't shut him off."

George Fraser's one problem was controlling his temper. Normally, he was a friendly, outgoing man who was known for his jokes. But when one of his three children stepped out of line once too often, George became an ogre. Hours later he settled back down to normality.

George got some help from a series of sermons on anger delivered by his pastor. He learned that anger is an emotion to be controlled and managed.

The pastor suggested several options that you can choose between when you get angry:

● You can suppress the anger, keeping it inside you. Some Christians do this, thinking they are spiritual. But actually they brood over their anger, and it usually takes its toll on them physically.

● You can ventilate and blow off steam. That was George's style. He felt fine after he was finished. But what about the hurt feelings and resentment his kids were left with?

● You can deal with your anger alone before God. Asking for God's grace, you can cancel out the resentment or hurt you feel. Ephesians 4:31 calls this "putting away" anger.

● You can let the other person know about your feelings of anger. When you do, tell him exactly how you feel, but do not criticize him personally. Just ask him to help you with your feelings.

George tried the fourth method with his youngest child, six-year-old Billy, and was amazed at the results. Billy respected his dad's feelings and showed a new attitude of obedience.

Anger is probably the most difficult emotion we must handle. Experiencing the emotion is human. It is not sinful. What is sinful is what we do with it when we lash out at somebody or harbor ill feelings about someone.

The Bible directs us to control our anger. Do not let it get out of hand or linger (Ephesians 4:26). Take your time getting angry (Proverbs 15:18; 16:32; 19:11; 29:11). When you are angry, decide what to do with your feelings (Colossians 3:8).

Most often anger results from having been ignored, mistreated, inconvenienced, or taken advantage of. You feel the urge to respond and correct the situation. Often this urge can be cancelled. Let God take care of it. Of course, if you are angry because of your child's disobedience, take care of the disobedience once you have your anger in hand.

On other occasions, you may not be able to get rid of the anger so easily. So express your anger to your child or wife. Tell him or her how you feel without assigning blame. Ask him or her to help you.

This approach gives your child a responsibility for you and changes his role from that of the accused to that of a helper.

"I won't remember half the things I'm supposed to do."

SIX

This Job Is Not Easy

This chapter is a coffee break. You have had five chapters of hard work. Your head may be spinning with all the information. This business of fatherhood is a huge responsibility. A small twinge of guilt may be there, too. You are not sure that you have been doing a good job.

If you feel overwhelmed and slightly depressed, take a few minutes to see where you stand. There are some big obstacles in front of you, obstacles as formidable as the front line of the Pittsburgh Steelers' defense. But you have an offense that can plow through and win.

What are the obstacles? The first is your own fear. You look at all the reasons that make you important as a father and you read all the suggestions on what you should do with your son. The questions fill your mind: *How can I do all this? I won't remember half the things I'm supposed to do. And I've probably blundered in many responsibilities.*

That feeling of despair is not new to any father. Sometimes it is easier to be ignorant of books like this and just do what you have to do. There are many successful fathers who have done exactly that. We take our hats off to them.

The secret of such fathers' success is their *involvement*. They build friendships with their sons and they spend time with them. If this book can help you to do the same, it is worth the money you spend. Take some or all of the suggestions to heart only if you need them. Do not worry about remembering or acting on them all.

The second obstacle is time, or your lack of time. Little more needs to be said. You know the problem.

A third obstacle is the subtle pressure in our society against being too serious a father. Whether you realize it or not, you live constantly with the pressure to keep fatherly activities to a respectable limit. Have you ever felt slightly embarrassed among your male friends for being too concerned about your children, for spending too much time with your family, or for refusing to participate in certain activities because of family obligations? Have you ever felt awkward visiting your child's nursery-school or grade-school function and finding yourself the only male parent in attendance? Have you ever read newspaper articles about fathers who live at home while their wives work, or male kindergarten teachers, or men who occasionally take their children to work with them, and wondered if you could do the same ? Have you ever observed a social gathering of couples and listened to the women talk about their children and the men about their jobs or their cars or anything but their own children?

Our society expects minimal involvement from fathers, and that is what it gets. Fatherhood is not a highly respected occupation. Rather, it is something men do when it is convenient or when they feel pressured by their wives.

WHY YOU CAN SUCCEED

The obstacles can slow you down, if not stop you in your tracks. But let's look at the powerful offense.

First, there is your desire to be a good father. If you sincerely want to be the kind of father this book describes, you probably will be. This is the *commitment* factor. When you are committed to being a good father, you make it a second full-time job or put it on an equal plane with your present salary-producing job. You give it the status of a calling in life that makes demands on your time, energy, and resources. You build your life around it. You take vacations from it to regain strength to do it better. You talk about it with your wife and friends. You put in overtime if necessary.

All this must affect your weekly schedule. On the following pages you will find a worksheet with explanations to help you see how you actually spend your time. If you are serious about this commitment, you can make the necessary changes.

Your offense gets even better when you consider your partner, that beautiful woman you married. Her role as mother is so influential; we do not have to make a case for that truth. She is also in your family to help you be a better father. You can delight her by simply asking her to help you. Have her read this book. Then work together on those areas of fatherly responsibility in which you want to improve.

The final member of the offense makes the victory certain. He is our heavenly Father. God's faithfulness to fathers from Abraham right down to our generation is one trust we can believe in more than any other. If you are part of His family, He is part of yours. He has a big stake in your family—He created it to fulfill His purposes.

So get back to work. You cannot lose.

TIME ANALYSIS WORKSHEET

	Subtotals	Totals	Priorities
PART 1—TOTAL HOURS IN A WEEK		168	
PART 2—REQUIRED TIME			
A. Average Weekly Hours—Sleeping	___		___
B. Average Weekly Hours—Family Support	___		___
Total of Part 2		___	
PART 3—AVAILABLE TIME (subtract Part 2 from Part 1)		___	
1. Working around the house, helping in the kitchen, repairing, building, shopping, driving people here and there, mowing the yard.		___	___
2. Watching television. (Be specific with yourself. Go day by day through the week.)		___	___

59

3. Eating. (Except meals taken during the hours you figured for family support.) ____

4. Church activities, including travel time. Worship services normally attended, Sunday school class, socials, choir practice, youth meetings, planning sessions. ____

5. Recreation with family, including going to concerts, sports events, playing games together, talking, studying, reading to or with, (but not television viewing). ____

6. Avocations, hobbies, special interests pursued without other family members, including community service, YMCA, service clubs, politics, bowling, golf, and so on. ____

7. With your wife. Going out together, talking, making love, praying and reading the Bible together, anything else you do, just the two of you together. (Television viewing is excluded unless you are actively discussing while you are watching.) ____

8. Reading books, magazines, newspapers. ____

9. Personal Bible reading, study, and prayer. ____

10. Bible reading, prayer, and other worship activities involving the whole family (at home, *not* at church). ____

11. Personal grooming, bathing, dressing, haircuts, conditioning. ____

12. Time alone with your son. ____

Total of Part 3 (This should be equal to the above total of available time.) ____

TIME ANALYSIS EXERCISE

PART 1

Every week contains 168 hours. How do you spend them?

PART 2

Sleeping. This item includes actual sleeping time only. Many people spend much more time in bed than they spend sleeping, and some sleep when they are not in bed. Do not include such possible in-bed activities as reading, praying, or watching television. Calculate very carefully to the nearest half hour how much time you are actually asleep during a typical seven-day week of the normal working year. Exclude vacations. Include Sunday afternoon naps, before- or after-dinner dozing, and any other regularly occurring sleep. Enter the average total for one week.

Family Support. This item includes any and all activities related directly or indirectly to supporting your family. It includes all the time from when you leave home until you return, plus any time you regularly spend at home, including doing such things as thinking, planning, phoning, or other "homework." Part-time jobs are also included. To this total for one week, add an average for such related things as union meetings, in-service training or other job-related education or study, golf with your business associates or prospects, and so on unless those things are part of the normal workday hours. Do not include any avocations—growing a garden, for example—unless they produce measurable monetary support for the family.

Add the two amounts—time spent sleeping and time spent in family support. This total normally accounts for almost all the time that is not available to be with the family.

Subtract that amount from 168 hours. The figure you get when you subtract is approximately the weekly time about which you must make the time-use decisions that directly affect your family and determine the way you fulfill your role as the Christian man in the family. This certainly does not suggest that what you do at work has no bearing on this family role; clearly, whether you succeed out there in the "world beyond home" is basic to your self-image and the image your family has of you. The time remaining after sleep and work is the time that you must allocate according to your personal priorities.

PART 3

Be careful not to put down what you think you should spend or wish you could, but only the amount of time that you actually

61

spend on each category of activity. Do not include your annual vacation here, although such events are certainly an important part of the overall picture. What we are after here is a review of your typical weekly schedule.

There may be some overlap for you in some categories, so be sure to count things only once. For example, gardening may be an avocation, recreation with the family, or working around the house, depending on how you do it and why. However, even though the whole family is together to watch television, that does not count as recreation with the family unless there is continual conversation during the program. By its nature, television tends to be an individual experience. Going to a ball game, on the other hand, tends to be a group experience even if you go by yourself, and even more so if you go with others.

Total the hours spent on the activities listed under part 3. Do not worry if you cannot account for all the hours in the week. This total should be the same as the amount of time remaining when the "required time" was subtracted from the 168 total hours in one week.

PERSONAL APPLICATION

In the column titled "Priorities," rank the activities in their order of importance to you. When you have completed the ranking, indicate by the use of arrows (↑ ↓) whether you should devote more or less time to each particular activity. Then decide how much more or less time you will spend (e.g., Watching television—three hours less) on each activity. Of special interest is the amount of time you decide to spend alone with your son.

PART 2

GET TO KNOW YOUR SON

Before you read Part 2:

The chapters in this part of the book are not an attempt to categorize your son, because that really cannot be done. Each boy is different. Some are slower and some faster than average in their development. Your son may never go through some of the stages identified as typical. However, in many respects, boys are more alike in their growing than they are different. Identifiable characteristics can be broken down into various age groupings.

This part will be much more valuable to you if you read the chapters immediately before and after the one on the age group your son is in now. For example, if your son is five years old, read chapters 8 and 10, as well as chapter 9. That will give you a much broader understanding of your boy because you will see where he has just come from and where he will soon be in his development, as well as where he is now. As you read, we hope these chapters will provide you with new and practical insights.

SEVEN

Your Son from Birth to One Year Old

YOUR WIFE AND YOU

As husband of your wife, you can contribute significantly to the well-being of your unborn child through the help and emotional support you give your wife. The emotional stability of the mother during pregnancy has direct effects on the emotional and physical stability of the developing fetus.

During the vulnerable stages of pregnancy, your wife will look to you, her provider and protector, to help her feel relaxed, confident, and secure. Reassure her that she is still attractive to you. Give her the needed sympathy for the aches and pains. Build her confidence in her competence as a mother.

When the baby comes home from the hospital, remember that this will have an effect on the relationship between you and your wife. You may have to be prepared to give up some of the attention your wife so freely gave you before the baby came. Your most important contribution at this point is to be a help, not a demanding burden to your wife. Be concerned with promoting your wife's emotional stability and security. She will then be a more effective mother and will love you more for it. This will naturally lead to a higher level of emotional health for your baby, as well.

HIS PHYSICAL GROWTH

Infant girls have proportionately more fat than boys, but infant boys have a greater proportion of muscle tissue than

"Come on son, don't you know this is part of your
Olympic training?"

girls and are usually heavier and longer at birth.

Your infant son has three basic physical needs, namely, *food, warmth,* and *sleep.* He will let you know when he is hungry. It will not be long before his mom (and perhaps you, too) can identify his hunger cry. These three basic needs are directly tied to your boy's emotional development and security.

Here is an illustrated guide to your boy's sequence of motor development. Remember, every infant is an individual. Some grow quicker than others. If your boy grows a little slower than another, it does not mean that he is any less normal.

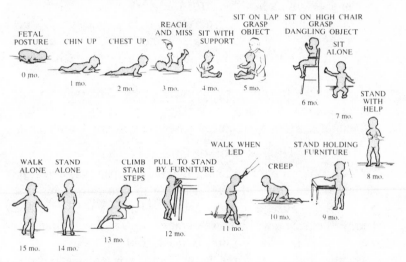

The sequence of motor development, with ages at which the average baby achieves each coordination.

Mary M. Shirley, *The First Two Years,* Vol. 2, University of Minnesota Press, Minneapolis. Copyright 1933 by the University of Minnesota.

By the time your boy is three months old he will begin to get teeth. That is part of the reason for his drooling, and teething may also cause some pain and discomfort and thus some crankiness.

When he can walk, your son will get into everything. He will love to explore, and he will be continually active and know few inhibitions.

WHAT YOU SHOULD DO

Get involved with your son as soon as he is born. Feed him, change his diapers, hold him, and play with him. If you do not know how to do these things, learn. It is not as difficult as learning how to tune a car or play golf. Your infant son's physical development is very much dependent on his sense of emotional security. He needs to know and feel he is loved so that he can grow into a healthy, strong boy.

You can help your boy develop his large muscles by encouraging his physical activity. Help him turn over, sit up, and grab onto things. Hold his hands and help him take some walking steps.

Be sensitive to your son's physical needs. The only way he can communicate when an infant is by crying (sometimes screaming). Hold your anger when he gets intolerable.

His Emotional Development

Your son's emotional health is largely dependent upon the climate of security and love available to him during his first year of life. His basic personality structure will be formed then. Whether he will be a self-confident or self-doubting person will be determined in his first year of life.

By the time he is three months old, your boy will smile readily. He will enjoy having you around and will vocalize in response to you by cooing and babbling.

By eight months, your boy will know how to express fear, anger, and pleasure. And by the time he is eighteen months old, he will know how to give and withhold love. He will still be "mamma's boy," but he may at times show a preference for his dad.

WHAT YOU SHOULD DO

Do not be embarrassed to cuddle and kiss your baby boy.

Your son needs to know you love him. If you want to show him you love him, the only way is by cuddling and fondling him. Infancy is the *ideal* time for you to build strong feelings of mutual love for your boy. Remember, this is essential for his emotional health.

Always be ready to respond to your boy when he reaches out to you. Too many dads communicate the attitudes, "I'm too busy," or "I don't want to be bothered," even at this early age.

Do not be concerned with spoiling your infant son with too much attention. It is nearly impossible to spoil your infant son with attention and love.

His Intellectual Growth

From the time your child is born, his mind is open to the whole world of sensory experiences. Whatever he hears, sees, touches, smells, or tastes is a new experience for him. He is learning at a rapid rate.

Explore, explore, explore: that is how your baby learns. At first he explores with his eyes. He will begin to recognize objects and people. He then explores with his eyes and hands; then with his eyes, hands, and mouth. When he begins to walk he will be into everything.

Your son's first form of communication is babbling and cooing. He will listen attentively to different sounds and begin to form and repeat certain vowel and consonant sounds. At eight months old he may begin to vocalize some words like "ma" or "da da." By the time he is eighteen months old, he may have up to twelve words or more in his vocabulary. He will understand far more words than he can speak.

By the time he is a year old, your boy will like to be read to. He will like picture books and be able to point out such objects as dog, cat, and cow. He will not understand all that you say and his attention span will be very short, but he will love the stimulation of sounds and pictures.

Whether your boy reaches his maximum potential intelligence depends to a great extent on how much sensory and intellectual stimulation he gets in the first five years of his life. Talk to him! Sing to him! Communicate with your baby boy!

When he can hold onto objects, give your son such things as plastic bottles, dishes, paper bags, blocks of wood, and chewable toys. Obtain or build a cradle gym or a mobile that can be hung above his head in his crib so he can handle it.

When he is old enough, begin to read to him. Begin with simple picture books and move up to short stories that he can understand.

Always be ready to provide your boy with new experiences. For the six month old, the backyard, with its pebbles, sticks, grass, and flowers, can be an exciting experience. The zoo is a great place for the one year old and older. The circus is a terrific experience for the eighteen month and older boy.

His Sexual Understanding

Your boy will begin to gain his sexual understanding even in this early stage of life. It begins with his growing understanding of his body. As he explores himself, he will discover his hands, feet, toes, eyes, nose, and so on. He will also discover his genitals and will become interested in them simply because they are a part of his body.

The discovery of his genitals has absolutely no sexual overtones to your infant boy, at least not in terms an adult would understand. On the other hand, how your son will feel about his sexuality later in life will largely be determined by your own attitudes about sex. It is important that you do not teach your son that his sex organs are "dirty" or something unusually different from the rest of his body. Allow him to discover and appreciate *all* of his body. When you find him playing with his genitals, do not react any differently than you would if you

70

discovered him playing with his toes. Modesty and privacy are things you will teach later in his life.

When your boy is able to say some words and you begin to teach him to identify parts of his body such as the eye, nose, and mouth, do not be embarrassed to teach him the proper names of his genitals. This is an essential beginning if you are going to have open communication between you and your son concerning matters of sex.

What He Can Learn Spiritually

This is the age of beginnings for your son. What he will learn spiritually also begins at this time of his life. If he is to be emotionally healthy, your son must know first of all that you love him. The feeling of being loved will also provide the foundation for his understanding of the biblical truth that God loves him.

As an infant, your son can learn what it means to *trust*. If he can blindly trust his parents for his basic needs, he will also some day be able to blindly trust God for his spiritual needs. This is directly related to his own sense of security, as mentioned under the discussion of his emotional development. Your ability to show your son gentleness, love, patience, and firmness may determine how your son responds to God later in life.

EIGHT

Your Son from Two to Three Years Old

At about the age of two, your son moves into an important transition in his development as a person. He is in transition from babyhood to childhood. This is a difficult stage in his development. It is difficult for your son because of the physiological changes he is experiencing, and difficult for you, the parents, because your little baby boy has turned into a "discipline problem."

Your boy at two experiences a time of marked disequilibrium (a state of imbalance between conflicting desires and interests). His favorite word is "no!" He often does not know how to make up his mind. He is often socially incompetent and intolerable. He may be inflexible and demanding. He may have violent temper tantrums. Many parents during this time experience feelings of inadequacy or failure as parents. Some parents react with harsher disciplinary methods; others throw up their hands in despair.

Your boy at two is beginning to learn about *self-identity* as opposed to *social conformity*. It is at this age that he strives to acquire a firm sense of selfhood—who he is as a person. However, at the same time he must learn to conform to what you, his parents, expect of him. That is why he does his best to express his independence while at the same time pushing you to set the boundaries for him. The results often seem chaotic, but do not give up. There is hope.

It is important at the outset to realize that most children go through this stage of disequilibrium. There is a reason for your boy's behavior. This does not imply that you are to do nothing about your son's difficult behavior. Discipline is necessary. Your own patterns of disciplining begin at this age. How you discipline is very important. More is said specifically about discipline later in this chapter and in chapter 14.

Much can be said on how to handle a "terrible two." The key is to be relaxed in your interaction with your son. You and your wife need to use great patience and express a real understanding of the difficulties of the age. This will get you through the stage more successfully, and when your son is into his third year, he probably will become a much more cooperative little person.

His Physical Growth

Your son at two and three is much more sure of himself in his movements than he was at eighteen months. He is less likely to fall. He runs and climbs more surely, though his coordination is not yet nearly as good as it will be later.

He is energetic, vigorous, and enthusiastic. He plays hard but tires easily and needs an afternoon nap, although he will probably refuse to take one.

He wants to learn to dress himself and has enough coordination to begin learning. However, his coordination may not be developed enough to give him easy success at dressing. This may cause frustration and outbursts of temper.

Into his second year, your son is probably ready to begin toilet training.

Your boy may experience some temporary crossing of the eyes at this age. Your boy may also be consistently sucking his thumb.

WHAT YOU SHOULD DO

Encourage your son's running and climbing. Play ball with him in the backyard. Run with him. Take him to the playground, and swing with him. Let him climb (if he wants to) up the steps to the top of the slide and then catch him as he slides down. If it is possible, set up a swing set or tire swing in your own backyard.

Encourage, *do not push,* his learning new skills such as dressing himself and brushing his teeth. In dressing, he will do better with familiar clothing that pulls on and off or has the buttons in front.

Toilet training involves teaching your child a new skill. Obviously, your wife will be the primary adult in this task, but you should be aware of how your wife is going about it. Here are some very basic guidelines.

• Wait until your son is ready, both emotionally and physically. Do not push him into it.

• Be *relaxed* and *patient* in your approach. If you are nervous about it, your boy will be, too.

• Start his training with his bowel movement. Bladder training will come later.

• Sit him on the "potty seat" only when you think he is ready to go or needs to go.

• If you were to teach your son a new skill like catching a ball, would you discipline him for his failures in catching the ball? Likewise, there is no place for discipline in toilet training, because it is simply teaching your son a new skill. He will have his failures and perhaps relapses. Be patient; he will learn if you give him the *positive reinforcement* he needs and ignore his failures.

If your son's eyes persist in crossing, perhaps you ought to seek professional advice. Thumb-sucking for a two and three year old is no cause for alarm. During these early years, it does not cause misshapen mouths. Thumb-sucking provides a sense of security for a child. If you are providing a relaxed, secure, and loving atmosphere for your son, he will stop his thumb-sucking before too long.

HIS EMOTIONAL DEVELOPMENT

Though your son is now beginning to "spread his wings" and express some independence, he is still emotionally dependent on his mom and dad for love, acceptance, and understanding. There are times when he needs you, his dad, to be affectionate with him. He still wants to know that you love him. Then there are times when he does not want your or his mother's affection—he is expressing his will to be independent.

During the first five years of his life, your son will develop his personality and his own self-concept. If he is going to be a self-confident person who knows how to get along with others, he needs *both* parents' assurance that he is a worthwhile person, even in spite of his negative and difficult behavior.

Your son expresses his emotional insecurities by crying, whining, fussing, and frequent questioning. He knows how to express strong opinions about some things. He can be very egocentric and think the whole world should revolve around him. He can become extremely jealous.

WHAT YOU SHOULD DO

Though your son wants to express some independence at this age, he still wants you to set the guidelines for him. He needs discipline and routine, but he needs you and his mom to be *flexible* and *patient*.

Show your love for your son both physically and verbally. He needs your emotional support as he grows out of babyhood into childhood. Do not be ashamed to give your son a big hug and kiss when he wants it.

Build your son's self-confidence by allowing him to express his opinions and his desire to try new things on his own. Build his self-worth with praise when he succeeds at something. Do not belittle your son by poking fun at his person or verbally attacking him for doing something wrong. You can express your disapproval for his *actions,* but do not constantly make him think that he is a failure.

Pay attention to your boy. If you are going to build a strong emotional relationship with your son that will last, now is the time to start. Be sensitive to his emotional needs, and be *patient*. At times it will be hard, but the dividends will be big.

How He Gets Along with Others

Your two and three year old can be a delightful companion. He loves being around his mom and dad and enjoys immensely getting involved with your activities. He loves to "help" his mom and dad do something. He can hold intelligent conversations with you on his level. He is still largely mom's boy, but he will want to spend special times with you, his dad, if you have encouraged such a desire.

Though the family is the center of his life, your son needs interaction with other people (adults and children) to build his awareness of the "outside world" and to teach him how to cope with its social demands. He is capable of giving affection to other adults and children. Depending on his own sense of emotional security, he likes to make new friends, though some shyness toward strangers can be expected.

People are important to your son. Relatives or close friends can be significant adult models who provide him with additional love and attention. Playmates are important, too. If he has no playmate, he may invent an imaginary one. He enjoys playing with another child, but his sociability is very limited. He is often very selfish and possessive of *his* toys. He can be shy one minute and domineering the next. If he gets frustrated with his playmates, he may react with kicking, hitting, screaming, biting, throwing, or a combination of these. He can learn to share, and sometimes he will use one toy to bargain for another.

Your son at this age generally can play side by side with other children. There are times when he can conform to the group, but at other times he is rigid and inflexible and will find it difficult to adapt, give in, or wait a little while.

If your boy has a brother or sister who is relatively close to his age, you can expect sibling fights, although he can express deep love and concern for his brother or sister.

WHAT YOU SHOULD DO

Actively build a strong bond of friendship with your boy. Although it will be more apparent later in your son's life, you are the major bridge between him and his success in the outside world. If he feels secure as a person and in his relationship with you, he will feel secure in stepping out and into new experiences in the world.

Be sure your son has plenty of opportunities to interact with other adults and children. He may feel secure enough to spend a night and a day at Grandma's and Grandpa's house. Special outings with other friends who have children his age will do much to broaden his social interaction. If circumstances will allow it, be sure your son has a playmate his age whom he can play with regularly. Sunday school and nursery at church will provide a good social environment for the interaction he needs with a group of children.

Be patient with your boy's unsociable actions. Gently teach him to share. He can learn to say please and thank you. He should know that biting, kicking, and hitting are not approved of, but remember that these are his immature ways of expressing his feelings. Be careful in disciplining his antisocial behavior not to force your boy to repress his feelings.

Your son's relationship with his brother or sister often tests your ability to be a fair and wise judge of who is right and who is wrong. Try to be impartial in handling sibling conflicts. Your son knows if you are showing favoritism either for or against him. Your son should have toys that everyone understands are his. Other toys can be designated to be "everyones" or as "belonging to the family." Encourage your son to share all these toys.

Your son's language ability is increasing. He can make known more clearly his wants and needs. He will begin to identify his world with words, and thus his world takes on new meaning. Your son may do some stuttering when he is three. That is not uncommon. If he is having unusual difficulty in expressing words, perhaps a specialist ought to examine him.

Play is serious business for your boy. He learns all about life through play. Play helps your boy assimilate new information. It helps him understand things better. When your son is involved in play, he is developing his mind because he is active in the process of thinking, reasoning, problem solving, talking, and imagining.

Your son loves to imitate. He will learn much about his world through imitation. He will pattern many of his own habits and ways of doing things after the ways of his mom and dad. He will imitate your way of brushing your teeth, wiping the table, sawing wood, mowing the lawn, washing the car, painting a wall, and so on. He will also imitate your ways of showing love and coping with tension.

Your son will naturally love the world of storybooks if you cultivate such a love. He can understand simple stories that have beginnings, middles, and ends. He loves to be read to because he loves words. He loves sounds of all sorts, especially unusual or funny ones. He enjoys the repetition and rhythm found in some nursery rhymes. He will have his favorite books that he wants read to him day after day.

Your son at this age can be very imaginative and creative. One way he will immensely enjoy expressing his creativity is through music. He loves to put music and gesture together. He can learn to sing, although he probably will not be able to get the right pitch in notes. He can memorize songs—especially those he can act out as he sings them. He responds to rhythm and loves to "dance" about when music is being played.

Your son is extremely curious about the world around him. Because he can now express his curiosity in words, such questions as "Why?" "How does it work?" "What is it?" will be a common part of his conversation. This continual questioning may at times be a nuisance, but if your son finds that it is all right to explore, that his questions will be answered, he will develop an inquisitive, adventurous approach to life that will be invaluable to him.

HOW TO STIMULATE HIS MIND

Learning to use language will be a significant intellectual stimulus for your boy. Introduce new words to him whenever you get a chance. Do not use baby talk with him. Play word games with him like "Label the Environment." He will be an enthusiastic participant in such games.

Your son will love activities such as painting, clay modeling, coloring, and building with blocks. Do these things with him and you will help stimulate his mind tremendously, as well as build a closer relationship with him. Be sure your son has a good variety of creative toys. Play with your son, make believe with him, and challenge his mind with new fantasies.

Remember that your son is a great imitator. He will love to imitate his dad if he feels that you love and accept him. He cannot pattern himself after anyone whom he does not think approves of or likes him. If you reject him, he will avoid you. That would be a direct hindrance to his intellectual growth. Involve your son in your activities. Let him help you do things. He may get in the way at times, but what you will be doing for his learning capacity and your relationship with him is worth the minor inconvenience.

If you want your son to do well in school, get him into books now. Find the time to read to your son. It will pay big dividends in his intellectual growth. When you sit and read to your boy, ham it up. Boys this age love to be dramatic. Use funny words and sounds, too. Let your son move the story along by asking him from time to time, "And what do you think happened next?" A good reference work on books for children from babyhood through adolescence is *A Parent's Guide to Children's Reading,* by Dr. Nancy Larrick. Ask your wife to see if she can get this book. Then together decide on some good books to get for your son.

Most record stores have children's music. Get your son a small record player and teach him how to use it. Some men find it difficult, but, if you can, sing with him. Sing action songs that use music and gestures together. Encourage him to memorize a simple song. Teach him the meaning of unfamiliar words. This may seem silly to you, but these activities do stimulate your son's mind, as well as provide him a fun experience with his dad.

Treat your child's questions with respect. Be patient and cultivate his attitude of wanting to know. Answer his questions simply, clearly, and without elaboration. Try not to explain too much. If your son wants more information, he will ask. If a particular question is one that can be answered by your son's seeing or doing something, that is the best way to explain, because children learn much from seeing and doing things for themselves.

A Word About Discipline

Your son is at an age at which you may feel pressured to better understand discipline. If you have not done it already, now is the time for you and your wife to discuss and evaluate your own approaches to discipline. There is no magic formula that works for every child, but it is important that you understand and implement some basic guidelines.

Discipline is a mother and father matter. You as father *must* realize that you have a significant responsibility to become involved in the raising of your children. Support your wife in her disciplining of your son. She should support you, as well.

Between you and your wife, look for a balance between

being too rigid and being too lenient in your expectations of your son. Your son needs guidelines for his behavior that are both consistent and flexible. Do not push or expect too much from your two- or three-year-old boy. Constantly evaluate his ability to do certain things.

Avoid anger and harshness. Be firm without being harsh. Even in discipline, let your love for your boy show through. Discipline and love are not antithetical; one is a function of the other. Do not hold a grudge against your child.

It is possible to control your son without nagging him. Warn him once clearly and firmly—maybe twice—but that is all.

A good, solid spanking is the best thing that could happen to some children. For other children, it is not. Spanking is not the cure-all disciplining method. It is so easy to strike out and hit a child, but it is a wiser parent who calmly analyzes the situation and follows through with the proper discipline.

Reinforce and reward your son for desirable behavior. Compliment him, make him feel good. Positive verbal reinforcement will strongly motivate your son to behave. It is human nature to want the approval of others. We all look for approval. Your son will look more and more for your approval if you are ready to give it to him.

What He Can Learn Spiritually

Your son believes most of what he hears, and thus he is completely open to spiritual truths. Now that you can converse with him in words, you can introduce some simple but significant spiritual truths.

He cannot understand symbols such as "the lost sheep" or "the bread of life." Nor can he understand spiritual concepts such as man's sinful nature, the Trinity, or that Jesus is both God and man. He will understand such concepts as love, trust, forgiveness, and the consequences of sinful actions, but they must be related to everyday experiences with which he is familiar.

82

Your son can know that God is the unseen Creator and that He is all-powerful, perfect, and our Provider. He can know that God is a real Person who loves and cares about him, even when he is bad. Your son can begin to say his own prayers when he is about three years old. He can begin to express his own love for God the Father and Jesus.

Your boy can identify with Jesus as a real Person and as someone who wants to be his best friend. He can know that Jesus is loving and caring, and that He came to earth a very long time ago, was a baby, grew up as a boy, and became a man. He can know that Jesus died on the cross, although he will not understand all the implications, and he can know that Jesus took our punishment for the bad things we do. He will not understand death very well.

Your son can learn that the Bible is God's book and that it teaches us how to be good. It also teaches us all we know about God and Jesus. He can understand and enjoy certain stories from the Bible if they are told on his level.

HOW TO HELP HIM GROW SPIRITUALLY

At this age your son will best learn of God's and Jesus' comfort, care, love, forgiveness, and protection by the way you provide him with these needs as his earthly father. Your relationship with your son, your other children, and your wife will leave a lasting impression on your young boy as he forms his early concept about spiritual things.

Get your son into the Bible. Bible storybooks are a good start. Show him a picture and build the story (on his level) around it, using your own words. Be sure to relate simple truths to his everyday experiences.

Pray with your son. Encourage him to pray. Prayer times should be both established—for example at bedtime—and spontaneous. Teach your son that praying is a natural and enjoyable time of talking to God. It is a time that pleases God, because He wants us to talk to Him. There will be times when your son is tired and cranky and may not want to pray with you. It is better not to force him to buckle under but to be an example and pray yourself. Remember, your son is a great imitator.

As was stated under "His Intellectual Growth," your son greatly enjoys music and rhythmic songs that utilize both words and gesture. There are many action songs your son will enjoy. They will teach him something about God and Jesus while at the same time associating spiritual things with happiness and joy. You and your wife can work together here. She can probably teach you some action songs if you do not know any. You can also make them up. Sing a song like "Away in the Manger," and make up your own gestures as you go along.

Look for everyday experiences in which God and Jesus can be mentioned naturally. Teach your son that God made the sun, stars, and moon. Whenever your boy becomes fascinated with a stone, stick, flower, or animal, ask him who made it. Teach him that God is the Provider of your home, food, toys, car, and everything else you have. Whenever you have the opportunity, bring God and Jesus into your conversation. Your son will soon come to realize that spiritual things are a natural part of everyday life.

NINE

Your Son from Four to Five Years Old

HIS PHYSICAL GROWTH

By the time your son is four, he has lost his baby fat and softness. He is a great deal sturdier. His larger muscles are growing rapidly. His legs will lengthen more rapidly than other parts of his body. This body growth results in better muscle coordination for running, jumping, and climbing. It also contributes to his increased physical activity.

Your four- or five-year-old son cannot sit still. He is constantly on the move. Instead of walking, he runs. Instead of closing the door, he slams it shut. If he can jump over something instead of walking around it, that is what he does. He often comes home with skinned knees and elbows, cuts, and bruises, but he heals fast. He enjoys using his physical skills. Often he comes to you and wants to demonstrate his abilities. "I can stand on my head, Dad. Want to see me do it?" This constant physical activity causes your boy to become easily fatigued and irritable.

Although his larger muscles are developing fast, his smaller muscles are growing, too. And although his smaller muscles do not function as dependably as the larger ones, your son enjoys activities that involve small-muscle coordination, such as buttoning, zipping, cutting, and painting with a large brush. He is probably not ready for writing skills. He can learn to dress himself, although he probably will find it difficult to learn to tie his shoes.

85

"Boy, dad, you bounce better than my bed!"

Your son's eyes are not yet fully developed. His eyeballs are still growing, and the eye muscles are not ready for much close work. Your boy may be somewhat farsighted and have difficulty with eye-hand coordination.

Most children by ages four and five are toilet trained. However, there are some children who for one reason or another develop a habit of bed-wetting. Boys are more apt to be slow in developing bladder control. If your boy at ages four to five is a bed wetter, remember that that is not highly unusual behavior. Any counselor at a young boys' camp will confirm that fact.

WHAT YOU SHOULD DO

If you can do nothing else to promote your son's physical development, play with him. Take him for a hike. Run with him, race him, wrestle with him. He can learn to throw and catch a ball or a Frisbee; encourage him in these activities. He can learn to ride a two-wheeled bike made for children of his size. Take some bike rides with him. These activities will help him develop his large muscle strength and coordination and fulfill his need to be on the go.

Get into the habit of taking your boy to the park (if there is one near you) once a week. Encourage his play on the swings, slides, and climbing apparatus, but let him do what he wants. He will be glad you are there to watch. If you are able, build your boy a tree house or a clubhouse of some sort. He will be glad to help you. If you have the right kind of tree, hang up a tire swing or just a good rope for climbing.

Since your boy is stronger and more coordinated than he was just a year ago, he can help you with some of the more physical tasks around the house like trimming the hedge, mowing the lawn, and cultivating the garden. He will need close supervision, but if you are patient with him, he will be glad to help, and you will help him greatly in developing his physical skills.

87

To help your son develop his smaller muscles, be sure that he learns to dress himself. Tying his shoes may be too difficult for him, but encourage him in his attempts. Playing with construction toys of various kinds is also very helpful to him. Encourage his painting and coloring efforts. You may want to sit down and play or paint with him. Such activities will not only develop his smaller muscles; they will also stimulate creative thinking. This is much better than having him watch television.

If your four- or five-year-old son has a consistent problem of wetting his pants, particularly during the day, you may want to have him checked by a pediatrician. However, in most cases, a boy bed-wetting at this age is just a little slower to learn self-control than most children. The best approach is to wait a while, and the problem will take care of itself. Sometimes a four- or five-year-old boy plays so hard during the day that he becomes overly tired and finds it difficult to wake at night to go to the toilet. Above all, do not belittle or ridicule your son for bed-wetting. That will often produce emotional insecurities that make it even harder for the boy to learn self-control. It may also destroy his confidence in you to support him through various problems he is facing.

HIS EMOTIONAL DEVELOPMENT

The four year old can display his emotions with great intensity. He may go into a fit of rage without notice. He can be brassy, boisterous, and shy, all in the same hour. His loves, hates, joys, sorrows, fears, and pleasures are all very close to the surface. Your four-year-old son, although he can verbalize his feelings, will most often express his feelings with his body by hitting, kicking, crying, laughing, whining, or using facial expressions. His emotional state at this point in his life can be wearing, both on him and on his mother.

Your five-year-old son, on the other hand, has better control over his emotions. He has learned to solve his problems in more acceptable ways.

Fear is probably the outstanding emotion four and five year olds have to live with. This fear deals with things both real and imagined. Real things such as trains, sirens, animals, and strangers produce fear in many children. A boy this age has a vivid imagination. Fear of the dark is common. Television violence can create fears. Even some fairy tales can make your boy afraid. The real and the make-believe are still hard for him to distinguish at times. Nightmares are also common at this age.

Your son is much more of an individual at this age. He likes to think that he is his own person. He has his own will in the true sense of the word. He is pushing toward more independence, but his emotional dependence on his parents, especially his mom, is still strong.

WHAT YOU SHOULD DO

If you are maintaining a close relationship with your son, you should be able to sense his need for your love and acceptance in spite of his lack of control with his emotions. Reach out to your son emotionally. He needs your support and reassurance about his worth.

You will inevitably need to use a good deal of firmness with your son between ages four and five. But try to maintain a balance between firmness and too much discipline. Your son does not need a repressive dictator. He will grow much better if he has a sympathetic father who allows him to express his feelings. This does not mean that you should exercise no control or allow him to be abusive of others. If you have been giving your son a sense of emotional security and guided discipline all along, you can be assured that his abrasive behavior now will pass as he grows.

In dealing with your son's fears, it is important to realize at first that many of his fears will come and go as time goes on. You cannot possibly deal with all his fears. Some of them he cannot even put into words. The best approach most of the time is to be sympathetic. Reassure him both physically and verbally that nothing is going to hurt him. Help him to talk about what he is afraid of, especially if he has just had a nightmare. As his father, you can be especially effective in helping your son with his fears because he generally looks to you as protector of the home. Please do not think that by making your son face his fears you will help him overcome them. If he is afraid of the dark, do not make him sleep in a dark room. If he is afraid of water, do not throw him into a pool unmercifully. He is not yet emotionally ready to face many of his fears head on, and he needs to be able to trust you to give him a sense of security.

HOW HE GETS ALONG WITH OTHERS

Your son at four or five has entered the world of friends. He consciously seeks out one, two, or even three children to play with in a small group. Often he quite abruptly excludes others from his group. He feels left out if others do not accept him.

Your boy is still very self-centered and individualistic. Bragging is a common form of communication. Name calling is also popular. He likes his friends, but he has not mastered social skills yet. He can be crude, blunt, and have (or show) little consideration for other people's feelings. However, as he mingles with other children, he is learning how to share, cooperate, take turns, and listen to others. He is learning that other people have rights, too. This kind of learning is of major importance in a child's life.

He is able to talk freely and express his ideas. He can be fun to talk with. He is full of wonderful plans. One of his greatest desires is to win the approval of adults. Sometimes, however, his means of getting attention are not acceptable.

By the time your boy reaches five he has acquired more social skills and gets along better with others. He often shares and is ready to take turns. He is learning to respect the rights and feelings of others.

Even though friends are becoming more important to your boy, he still greatly appreciates and depends on friendship with you. You as his father will be a key factor in his ability to develop social skills. How well you get along with him will greatly determine how well he gets along with his peers.

Be sure that your son is interacting with some children of his own age. He will gladly play with either girls or boys, but he probably prefers boys as friends. There may be some children in the neighborhood whom you do not want your boy to play with, but for the most part it will do your boy good to associate with neighborhood children. If there is a Christian family nearby with a boy of the same age, friendship between the two boys would be ideal.

You can help your son develop his social abilities, but most of them will develop naturally. If your son comes home for supper some evening with a black eye that was administered by four-year-old Johnny down the street, you can help your son resolve that conflict by going to Johnny's home after you eat and, in a relaxed manner, talking over the problem with Johnny, his dad, and your son.

HIS INTELLECTUAL GROWTH

A boy at age four and five is eager to learn, and he now has a much greater capacity for it. His curiosity and imagination will drive him to learn and absorb all he can about his world and the people around him. Over 10 percent of his speech is made up of questions.

Your son has a heightened interest in language. He is fascinated by words and sounds of words, and he likes to make up silly words and rhymes. He probably has a vocabulary of fifteen hundred to two thousand words at ages four and five, and he understands a great many more. He often uses words he does not understand.

A boy four or five years old is literal minded. He accepts

91

words and phrases he hears at face value; he cannot understand idioms. Symbolism and other figures of speech are also confusing to him.

Your son's imagination is very vivid. Sometimes he cannot distinguish between what he imagined and what is real. He can pretend to be any character he wants to be. He loves to make up stories. Imaginary companions are common at this age.

Curiosity motivates your boy at this age to learn all he can about the people, things, and events around him. He wants to know about everything. He asks questions continually. He wants to know how and why something works. He enjoys explanations that help him think through simple cause and effect. He can reason with true logic. Curiosity drives your boy to explore everything. He will drag home all sorts of things he has collected. This is his way of experimenting and learning.

Your son's play is an important means of learning. He loves to play house, doctor, store, and other games that simulate adult life. In this dramatic play he is relating himself to and testing his world, trying out his role, and expressing his feelings about his relationships with other people. He is learning to solve problems as he acts them out in make-believe play.

Your son continues to love stories. If you have not begun a regular time of reading to your boy, now is a good time to start. Cultivate his love for books and you will do a great deal for his intellectual abilities in school. He enjoys pictures and stories about the familiar world around him. He likes a story of about three hundred to four hundred fifty words that is full of action and repetition. He has his favorite stories and often acts them out.

Most children at ages four and five are ready or almost ready for school. Your four year old might profit from going to nursery school; consider sending him if you can afford it. A nursery school is a children's world rather than an adult world: it will provide your son with activities that a home cannot provide that will help him develop both physically and intellectually. Participating in guided activities with other children also promotes his social skills. Five year olds should enter kindergarten. School experiences are probably just what your child needs to help him mature, but this is not a hard and fast rule.

HOW TO STIMULATE HIS MIND

Ages four and five are two of the best years for your child to learn how to learn. The more intellectual stimulation you give to your boy now, without pushing or pressuring him, the brighter and more intelligent he will become. You need to provide a mentally stimulating atmosphere in your home. This begins with a careful selection of toys, games, books, and records. Check the resource section on pages 189-204 for some ideas.

Using clear and simple speech with your boy will help his language development. Stories both read and told become increasingly important. The best kind of books are those with stories about things that are real to him, as opposed to fairy tales. Books about animals that act like people are especially interesting to him. He never tires of stories about other children, or even about himself. He loves to discuss the stories he just heard.

Be patient with your son's curiosity. Give simple (not too simple) answers to his questions in terms he can understand. To stimulate his curiosity, take him to various interesting places. These do not have to be complicated trips. A ride to the railroad station, to the lot where a new apartment building is going up, or to a friend's home where there are some new puppies will be of great interest to him. Build a large box in which he can store his collections of things. Talk with him about things he has collected. Every once in a while you can help him clear out items in which he is no longer interested.

Your son is capable of a great deal intellectually—perhaps more than your realize. This may be a good reason for sending him to nursery school, the benefits of which were discussed previously. But you and your wife know your son better than anyone else. You must be the ones to evaluate whether nursery school would be good for him. One thing is sure: not sending him to nursery school will not hurt him. Talk the decision over with your wife, and put it to prayer.

HIS SEXUAL UNDERSTANDING

In connection with your son's increased interest in language, you may be shocked to hear him use some four-letter words and "bathroom language." He will discover the shock value they have. Sometimes those words are funny to him. Often, he uses those words because he assumes they are a badge of being "grown up." Nothing is gained by acting shocked or horrified. Try to remain relaxed, but let him know in no uncertain terms that the use of such language is not acceptable and is bad manners (like sticking out his tongue).

Your son may find it fascinating to engage in play that is clearly sexual in nature. You may find him playing "doctor" or "nurse" with some little girls, games in which they will be removing clothing and touching each other in an intimate way. Sometimes both boys and girls at this age invent peeping games in which they show off "interesting" parts of the anatomy. This kind of play is related to your son's curiosity. He wants to know what a girl looks like and see what his own emerging sexual feelings mean. The best way to prevent excessive sexual play is to keep communication open between you and your son. If you perceive that he is curious about sex, talk freely about it with him. Welcome his questions. He needs only basic information. Most of all, be calm but firm in limiting sexual play. Try not to harm his natural interest in sex and love.

You may discover your son fondling his genitals. (Even at this age, he can be sexually stimulated to some extent by such activity.) This fondling is not at all uncommon. It will not harm him physically. The best approach is *not* indignation, making him feel guilty or as though he is participating in a dirty act. Instead, try to divert his attention to other activities.

94

Being open and honest about sexual matters is extremely important to your son. He is just beginning to assimilate the reality of relationships, the differences between boys and girls, and what that all means. He is often confused. He may pick up distorted information from schoolmates and neighborhood friends. He needs you to be ready to answer his questions. Where do babies come from? How does a baby get inside Mommy? How do babies get out? Can I have a baby, too? These are just a few of his many questions. Answer them as simply as you can, without great elaboration and in terms he understands. If you have been teaching him the proper names of the anatomy, including genitals, explanations about sex will be easier.

WHAT HE CAN LEARN SPIRITUALLY

Your son at four and five can think of God in a personal way. He understands that God is perfect and the Creator. He senses God's greatness and wonder. He can associate God with things that are good, true, and beautiful. It cannot be emphasized enough, however, that much of your son's concept of God the Father is related to his relationship with you. Can he trust you? Can he depend on your love and discipline? Do you show love to him in spite of his shortcomings? If you can say yes to these questions, then you have profoundly helped your boy develop a better sense of who God is.

Your boy can deal with Jesus as a personal friend. He can understand that Jesus is God's son, but he will not understand the concept of the Trinity.

Your son at this age is gaining a deeper understanding of the difference between right and wrong. His conscience is emerging. He can know his wrong actions are sin in the eyes of God. He can feel sorry for his sin and confess it. If you have expressed genuine forgiveness of his wrongdoings, he can better experience God's forgiveness. He needs to understand that God loves him even when he is bad.

Your son at age four or five can become a Christian in the

95

true sense of the word, but let him grow into this in his own time. Too many parents have pushed their children into a decision for Christ when the children were not really ready both intellectually and spiritually. A child will often naturally come to the Lord, although he may not be able to identify a specific moment of decision.

The Bible can and should become an interesting and important book for your boy. The Living Bible is easy to read, and your son will be able to understand much of the narrative. A picture Bible storybook is also excellent. Cultivate a time each day for Bible reading with your son. This will do much toward developing his love for the Word.

Your son can worship in a very real sense. He is naturally fascinated by new things he discovers each day. When his fascination and wonder are directed toward an appreciation of God and His greatness, worship becomes very natural and real for him. He finds it easy to pray and talk to God if you have encouraged him. He may not understand God's invisibility, but he believes he can talk to Him. Singing and praising God is natural for your boy. He loves rhythms and action songs. It may be difficult for you to sing with him, but you can probably count on your wife for help.

TEN

Your Son from Six to Seven Years Old

HIS PHYSICAL GROWTH

You already know that your son is *active*. That one word describes the way he lives and what he likes. His large muscles are developing rapidly, and they demand to be used. Wrestling, running, jumping, climbing, kicking, throwing, and catching are all popular for this reason. His whole body is involved in everything he does.

Your son often does not know when to slow down. He gets tired easily because his heart is not fully developed, and he pushes himself beyond his capability. Afternoon rest periods are still needed for most boys, as is a good night's sleep (eleven to twelve hours).

He enjoys making things with his hands. Carpentry, building simple models, painting, and learning to use some hand tools are enjoyable to him. He does get frustrated with failure in these projects because his hand-eye coordination is not complete, and the small muscles of his arms and hands are not fully developed.

His baby teeth have already begun to come out and be replaced by permanent teeth. Molars also appear. Sore gums may cause him to be irritable. His eyes are still not mature in either size or shape, and their relatively shallow depth probably causes some continuing farsightedness.

He is able to develop good health habits: brushing teeth, combing hair, taking a bath, changing clothes, washing hands

"Wait a minute, dad, I have to go to the bathroom!"

and face before meals, and eating balanced meals with good manners.

WHAT YOU SHOULD DO

Play with your boy. Get down on the floor and wrestle with him. Try every sport you can think of. Take him on a hike. You will get the exercise you need in the process. Be sure he has plenty of opportunity and space for the free and active play he needs. Be patient with his inability to stop wiggling. He may try hard to sit still, but he will be unable to do so for long because he will have difficulty controlling his movements voluntarily.

Build things with him and allow him to help you with household projects. Watch out for projects that are too complicated. Encourage him to do as much by himself as he can. Be patient, however, remembering that his physical development has a long way to go before he can master many skills.

You need to support your wife in teaching your boy good health habits, but avoid nagging him about his inconsistencies or inability to do certain things. Be sure he visits the dentist to get his new teeth off to a good start.

His Emotional Development

Your son's life is not all fun and games. He has a great need for acceptance and approval. Criticism is what he *does not* need but often gets. Criticism from adults usually hurts him deeply. His emotions are intense. He experiences deep feelings of worry, fear, frustration, and resentment.

He gets discouraged easily. He does not like to make mistakes or fail in a project. His temper can flare easily. He has a need for reassurance and encouragement. He is trying to be independent, but he avoids new and difficult situations for fear of failure.

His vivid imagination may cause him to have fears of scary

creatures or strange people, or of being deserted by his family; fear of the dark may also reappear at this age.

He needs to feel secure in his own world. Adults are the source of his sense of security. How you and your wife handle problems and tensions makes an impact on him. Your son will enjoy demonstrations of love and affection by his parents while at home, although he may be shy about it in public.

You are the most important human being in his life right now! He is deriving much of his own identity from his imitation of you. Your son is developing his own concept of manhood at this age. Child psychologists call it "sex role development." He is learning from *you* what it means to be a man, father, and husband. He will covet the times you spend alone with him. Your criticism or rejection of him can devastate him. Your firm leadership can stimulate him tremendously.

WHAT YOU SHOULD DO

Spend time alone with your boy. Take him places with you. Talk with him. In your boy's overall development toward manhood, this is one of those particular ages when he needs you to be close by him. Building a friendship with him now will not only enable you to be a better father to him at this age, but it will also provide a base of love and understanding between the two of you that will better carry you through his difficult adolescent years. One good way to spend regular time with your son is to join a Christian Service Brigade Tree Climbers program. Designed just for boys six and seven and their dads, this program will do much for his emotional and social development, as well as help you build a close relationship with him. An alternative program, although it is a secular alternative, is the YMCA's Y/Indian Guides program.

Encourage your son to confide his insecurities and hurts to you. This takes sensitivity and sympathy on your part in discussing matters that may seem trivial to you but are serious to your boy.

Evaluate your expectations of your son. Are you requiring too much, so that he thinks he is constantly failing? Are you forcing him into roles for which he is not yet ready? Look for and recognize the positive things he does. This does not mean you should always ignore the negative. It simply means you put your emphasis on the positive, not the negative. Constant criticism will make him feel worthless and insecure.

Show a lot of love to your boy. This should come through your actions, as well as verbally. Many dads find this difficult. Swallow your pride and come right out and tell your son you love him. It will pay high dividends in your relationship with him.

Be consistent, firm, and fair in your dealings with your son. This will give him a secure and happy state of mind. When tense situations occur in the family, remember your boy is watching your reactions. You need to exhibit self-control and leadership.

How He Gets Along with Others

Although your son's primary loyalty is to his family, he is becoming sensitive to the attitudes of his friends. He can be influenced easily by them. His friendships will expand because he is starting school. Since he has more friends to choose from, he may shift quickly from one child to another. He enjoys being the center of attention and will show off or make smart remarks to make an impression. His self-centeredness will often show when he is with friends. Name-calling is a method of defense or attack that he may use. He prefers to play with other boys, but he will play with girls, too.

Your six- or seven-year-old son will often idolize an older, teenage brother. Brothers and sisters who are close in age tend to compete with each other; rivalries will occur, but brothers and sisters can also be the best of friends. Sisters of almost any age are usually in for a rough time. Your son is apt to tease them. It will be quite normal if he wants nothing to do with preschool brothers or sisters. They are a nuisance as far as he is concerned. You will soon discover that your boy is able to "dish it out" better than he can take it.

Your son does not consciously realize it, but he needs to experience what other adults are like. As his parents, you and your wife are his primary examples. Exposure to adults of other races, ages, backgrounds, and occupations will give him a wider perspective on life as he is reaching out to learn more about the world around him.

Your son's schoolteacher is very important to him. If he is having trouble getting along with his teacher, you will need to step in. On the other hand, he may claim he is "in love" with his teacher if the teacher is a woman.

At six and seven years old, your son is beginning to break away from his mother's apron strings; this may cause conflicts between him and your wife, or at least periods when he is antagonistic and disobedient. Those times will be interspersed with periods of warm friendliness, when he treats his mom like a girlfriend.

WHAT YOU SHOULD DO

Show interest in your son's friends. Talk to him about them. Encourage him to invite his friends home, and make an effort to be friendly toward them. Your son is probably very proud of you, and he will greatly appreciate your interest in his social life. Your son's friendships may be shifting from neighborhood children to newly found school friends. Do not be overly concerned about his lack of loyalty to former friends. Such loyalty will develop in a couple of years.

Avoid comparing your son or pitting him against his brothers and sisters. Teach your boy to treat other family members with love and fairness. This will require some patience because of his immaturity. He needs firm guidelines, but you need to strive to treat him fairly, too, particularly in sibling disagreements. Your son eagerly seeks your approval. He will be watching closely how you give approval and discipline to his brothers and sisters, and he will invariably compare your treatment of him with your treatment of your other children.

See that your son gets a regular chance to interact with other adults on a level that is meaningful for him. Grandparents, uncles, or cousins are good for this. Be sure to treat your son with respect when you are with other adults. Let him speak for himself, and listen to him as you do to others. Do not let him dominate a discussion, however. It is important that your son feels he belongs in the world of adults. This will help build his sense of security and his sense of identity.

Get to know your son's schoolteacher. You will be surprised at how much influence a teacher can exert on your son. He or she probably spends more time with your boy than you do during the school year. Your son's teacher will form definite opinions about his abilities. His or her opinions may not always be accurate. Meeting you will help him or her to better evaluate your son. And a teacher will often offer valuable insight into your son's developmental needs.

His Intellectual Growth

Your son is an eager learner. His world is expanding through school. He still asks many questions. *Why* is a favorite word. However, he will learn better by participating than by sitting and listening. He needs to feel, see, do, and experiment. Make-believe play is still a strong part of his learning process. His love for dramatization carries over from play to conversation. Your son loves to tell a story using gestures, often moving his whole body expressively as he talks.

Your son's language abilities develop quickly between ages six and seven. He uses a vocabulary of about three thousand words. He understands the specific, concrete meanings of words, but not the abstract meanings. He loves to talk and will often talk on and on just for the pleasure of it. His discussions revolve primarily around his family or around himself and the things he has done. His ability to use language to express his feelings and problems has increased.

Your boy still loves a good story. His attention span has increased so that he sits and listens longer. He can stay with a continuous story read from day to day over a period of time. Now that he is beginning to read for himself, he will enjoy reading some stories on his own. But mostly he still likes to be read to. His reading interests include animal stories, adventure stories with boys in them, imaginary fables, stories with comic-book characters, and action-packed stories from the Old Testament.

Your son's interest in stories carries over to television. He may come dashing home from school, eager to watch some of his favorite programs. Remember that your son's mind is like a sponge. He absorbs much more than you might realize. However, much of the information he gets from television will be distorted or confusing because he relates what he sees to his limited experiences. A broader spectrum of information may be one benefit of some television programs, but too much television viewing may undermine your son's ability to think creatively. Passiveness may be another of the worst effects of excessive television viewing.

Most boys have little difficulty entering first grade and adjusting to the school routine. However, for some boys it can be a threatening experience. Your son will now be expected to perform in his schoolwork in a way that is more demanding than kindergarten work. Getting behind in schoolwork or simply not enjoying the daily routine can deeply affect him. Since his school habits are being formed now, close observance of how he is doing is important if you are going to help him over the rough spots. If he has a rough start, he will most likely do much better by the time he reaches age seven.

Your son may be ready for a small allowance. He can learn the names of the various coins and how they relate to each other. He should learn about saving, spending, and giving.

He can learn to put aside a portion of his allowance for the Lord.

WHAT YOU SHOULD DO

Your son is a natural doer, and he will greatly enjoy doing things with you. Try to find the time to initiate various kinds of interesting projects with him. Here is a handy formula to keep in mind: your son learns 90 percent of what he does and 10 percent of what he hears. He learns 50 percent of what he sees someone else doing. He naturally looks to you as an important source of information and answers to his many questions. His eyes will open wide as you challenge him with a new piece of knowledge about the world around him. You can stimulate his questioning mind by asking him questions. He needs to know that it is all right and good to question, explore, and experiment. At times it will be difficult to be patient with his questions, but if you can succeed in encouraging his inquiring mind, you will do much to give him the sense of security he needs to step forward into new experiences and discover his world.

One of the best ways to help your son grow intellectually is to encourage his language development. You need to help him articulate what is on his mind, and the best way to do that is to listen patiently to him. Much of his ability to learn how to express himself is dependent on how well you and your wife genuinely listen to him. This is an important step toward good communication between you and your boy. He is probably a great talker, especially at age six. Help him to pronounce words correctly. He will often use a word whose meaning he does not really know. Help him clarify the meanings of words. Be concerned with how he expresses himself verbally, but also show interest and concern in what he is saying and in his underlying emotions.

Reading is a new adventure for your boy in these years. He enjoys reading for himself. He still enjoys being read to. Regular periods of reading out loud can be very stimulating. Your participation, listening to him read and reading to him, will pay rich benefits in his later years. If encouraged, he loves to dramatize many of the stories he hears. This helps him better assimilate the information and concepts the stories teach. Your son also enjoys creating his own stories. Encourage him to do this. Have him tell his stories to the whole family.

Television is a major influence on your boy's mind. It should be controlled. Your son will probably enjoy these kinds of television programs: action stories with police or firemen, cartoons, programs with young children in them, situation comedies with popular characters, and football and baseball games. Take the time to watch some of these (the ones you approve) with him, and talk about them later. Use them as opportunities to teach spiritual and moral truths.

One way *not* to stimulate your son's mind is to push him for academic achievement. Such pressure can have an effect opposite to what you intended. Allow your son's teacher to encourage his academic achievement. It is his or her job to know what he can and cannot absorb in school.

It is important to your boy that his dad have a positive and active attitude about school. He will probably have the same attitude about school that you have. Is your attitude complacent and uncaring? Then very likely your son will be complacent and uncaring.

Your son will attend one of several kinds of schools: (1) traditional classroom; (2) open classroom; (3) computerized learning programs; or (4) some variation of one of these. Each has its strengths and weaknesses. Learn what they are as they relate to your son. Attend PTA meetings and teacher-parent conferences. Visit the classroom once. The teacher will welcome you. If your job will not permit this, at least remember the name of your son's teacher. That will mean a lot to your boy. Make school functions in which your son participates a top priority in your schedule. Always show an interest in what he brings home from school. Look for something you can praise.

HIS SEXUAL UNDERSTANDING

Your son has an increased awareness of sexual differences between boys and girls. He and other children his age may still engage in sexual play by showing each other various parts of the anatomy. Sexually oriented jokes are common on the school grounds. In most cases, however, a boy's sexual interest at this age begins to tone down and become more hidden from adult eyes. Your boy may masturbate, but it will be less frequent and more private than when he was younger. Your son needs for you to maintain an open policy on discussions about sex. He still has many sex-related questions. You should be the one giving him the basic information he needs. This will help him have a healthier attitude about sex. He will not feel as inclined to hide his interest from you. He will also be less apprehensive and embarrassed about what he does not know.

Training on modesty should begin at this age. Your son may feel a need for privacy, and that should be respected. It is recommended that you and your wife do not expose your nakedness to your six- or seven-year-old boy. This does not mean you should hide in embarrassment if he walks in on you. Simply explain that you prefer to be alone when you are bathing.

It is to be hoped that by now you have cultivated some honest and matter-of-fact communication between you and your son concerning sexual questions. If you and your wife are embarrassed to discuss sex, your son will more than likely be overly curious or very apprehensive himself. In a society in which sexual stimulation is everywhere, it is best to be open with your boy and in a relaxed manner encourage his questions. He will have questions about the origin of babies, the process of birth, the father's part in reproduction, the sex organs and their functions, and marriage. Too much detail is unnecessary and can be confusing in answering his questions.

107

It is better to respond with simple answers that contain the basic facts. Be sure to use correct terminology, including the proper names of genitals, when discussing sexual matters with him.

In school, sex education usually begins with the study of animals and plants and moves on to the study of the family and community. Sex education is not a separate subject, but instead is part of the total curriculum in science, health, and social studies. You can help your son by being aware of what he is learning in school and providing him with supplemental information through children's books about reproduction in animals. Books that provide pictures of the anatomy and the fetal stages are also helpful for good discussion between you and your boy. See the resource section on page 199 for some suggestions on books. If you could somehow arrange for your son to witness the birth of some animal, he would not only find it fascinating but he would also learn to understand and profoundly appreciate birth.

What He Can Learn Spiritually

Make God a constant subject in your conversation. He is a real Person who is part of your family life. Your son will probably ask where God is and why He cannot be seen. His understanding of God will remain somewhat vague in spite of your explanations. But he can understand some basic truths about and attributes of God.

He can understand that God loves him, his family, his friends, and all the other people in the world as well. He can know and appreciate God's forgiveness for wrongs that he has committed. He can understand that God's omnipotent power can make a person well or calm a storm. Stories in the Bible that show God's power are exciting to him.

Your son can have a personal relationship with Jesus. He knows that he has committed sin (although the concept of a sinful nature is too abstract for him) and that this is not pleasing to God. He can understand and believe that God forgives

108

him because Jesus accepted the punishment for his sin on the cross. He can also invite Jesus into his life and know that he belongs to God's family and will live with God forever in heaven.

Do not pressure your son into a formal conversion experience. Let him initiate the decision himself. Concern yourself with providing him with sound Christian teaching that will prepare him to respond to God's call. Let him share in your (and your wife's) relationship to Christ by encouraging him to pray, read the Bible, and obey God's commands. Pray for him daily, and let him know that you are praying for him.

You can play a vital role in your son's relationship to Jesus. Have a time of "personal devotions" with him each day. Talk to Jesus with him. Talk about some Scripture with him and relate the Word to specific situations in his life. He should have a children's Bible of his own.

Remember that biblical truth is best communicated relationally. This means that your example and the loving relationship you build with your son will convey more scriptural truth to him than long family devotions in which you lecture. Concentrate more on helping him understand concepts (e.g., what it means to love our enemies; what is meant by God's omnipotence) than on having him learn and memorize facts about the Bible (e.g., how many chapters there are in the book of Acts).

ELEVEN

Your Son from Eight to Eleven Years Old

His Physical Growth

Your son is still full of energy. He still loves to shout, climb, rough and tumble, wrestle, and play tag, although he also now enjoys organized games with rules. He is, on the whole, much more robust than when younger and he is very self-assured about his bodily coordination.

His body is still growing, but the growth rate has slowed considerably now. It will pick up again to a more rapid pace when he reaches adolescence. Hand-eye coordination is definitely improved. Previous farsightedness should be gone, but many children develop some nearsightedness at this age. If your son is tall or thin for his age, he may develop some posture problems.

During this age period, your son's permanent teeth will appear. He also has a growing desire for tooth-rotting candy, gum, and pop. Toothbrushing habits need to be carefully maintained at this time.

Your son's small-muscle development has advanced considerably. He can write much more evenly than he could earlier, and he can do craft work with tools that require skillful manipulation. He likes to do things well and wants to learn new skills.

Because he is still so physically active, your boy needs regular hours for going to bed and rising. Happy mealtimes and well-chosen foods for nutrition are essential for his health.

Be proud of son's new physical abilities. He loves to hear your praise. Encourage your son in organized sports if that fits his needs, but also allow him to develop interests in other areas as well. Please do not be fooled by the misconception that to be a "real boy," your son must be athletic.

Your son loves to learn new skills. He will have the opportunity to do so at school, but there is no reason you cannot teach him some physical skills if you will take the time to play with and encourage him. Do not push your son to meet your preconceived expectations. Love and accept your boy for the abilities he has, and gently encourage him to develop them at his own pace. Some of the things you can teach him are how to pitch a ball, dribble a basketball, swim, ride a bike, and hunt. If you enjoy arts and crafts, teach your boy craft-related skills. You can also teach him workshop skills like using saws, hammers, files, wrenches, and other tools. Much of what you teach him should center on your own physical skills and interests.

Your son may not exhibit much physical prowess. He may be somewhat clumsier or weaker than most boys. This may result in his being excluded from certain groups and games boys play, and it will put a good deal of emotional stress on him. Just because your boy is not the "physical type" does not mean that he is any less normal, or a "sissy." He needs his dad's assurance that he is just as much a boy as any of his peers. Encourage him in other kinds of activities in which he may be more successful. If he earnestly wants to learn athletic skills, patiently work with him and teach him what you can.

Sending your son to a summer camp will also do much to develop his physical and social skills. Encourage him to join a boys' club if there is one in your area. The activities in those clubs are successfully built around boys' physical interests and abilities. You may even want to consider becoming a leader in one of those boys' clubs.

His Emotional Development

Your eight-to eleven-year-old son is moving toward adulthood. He knows he is still a child, but at times he likes to think of himself as an adult. He does not like to be referred to as a little boy or a child. He is increasingly able to take care of himself. He feels more secure in taking long trips away from home. He can also take on more responsibility. He should be able to keep his room clean, take care of his own pets, and be able to handle some household chores. He is not consistent in fulfilling his responsibilities, however.

Boys this age enjoy competitive games, and some competition is good. However, your boy may not be emotionally able to handle intense competition. Winning can become too important. Losing can cause him to feel like a total failure.

Your boy may tend to be a perfectionist at this age. He wants to do things right. Sometimes he sets out to do things beyond his capabilities or sets standards for himself that are too high. Failure to reach his goals will cause him to be very self-critical. He can be overly conscientious and begin to worry. He can develop a genuine fear of failure.

Your son at eight to eleven years old is better at controlling his emotions than he was when he was younger, but he still can get angry and lose his temper. He may express some rebellion against your authority. He may rebel by withdrawing or complaining. His rebellion is probably just part of his emotional development, as is the case with most boys at this age. On the other hand, his rebellion may be the result of your expecting too much of him, or it may be the result of some other emotional strain in the family.

Your boy's sense of humor is very lively. He can laugh at himself, and he is quick to pick up absurd statements and words. His humor is slapstick and hearty. He laughs when an authority figure looks silly. This gives him a sense of superiority. He enjoys surprise, especially in the form of practical jokes.

113

Try to treat your boy as though he is mature, even though he is not consistent in being so. Do not talk down to him as though he were still a little child. Be sure that he gets some new responsibilities that are important to him; give him choices when you can. Let him take turns with household jobs. Reward him with praise for work well done. Do not criticize him for his inconsistencies, but do gently encourage him to follow through with his responsibilities.

Competitive games can be good for your son. This is an excellent age for him to learn sportsmanship. You cannot eliminate competition completely anyway, because he will naturally compete, even in his spontaneous play. Team against team is better than one-on-one competition for your boy. Do not be the kind of father who overly pushes his boy to be competitive. That can be harmful and may someday backfire on you. Be sensitive to your boy if he prefers or needs to be excluded from game play. He will need your emotional assurance that he is a worthy person.

Although your son is now more influenced by friends and teachers than he was when younger, he still very much depends on his parents' love and emotional support. That love is an important base for him as he strives to succeed in an often-harsh world. Do you consider him to be a worthwhile person in spite of his shortcomings? If you do, tell him so. Do you push your son to meet your expectations of what you think he ought to be, or do you allow him to be his own person and encourage him in the directions he wants to go? For your son's sake, you should take the latter approach.

Maintain a friendly relationship with your eight-to-eleven-year-old boy. Be able to laugh and share in fun experiences with him. If you can model a relaxed approach to life in general, your son will be able to do the same. He will then be able to handle better some of the emotional turmoil he experiences at this age. That will in turn better prepare him to deal with the difficult adolescent years.

How He Gets Along with Others

Your son has come to an age at which he evaluates himself in relation to others. To a degree he can evaluate his own weaknesses and strengths in relation to others' strengths and weaknesses. Your son will look for a best friend if he does not already have one. His ability to make and keep friends has greatly increased.

This is the age for "gangs" of the same sex. Your boy will often refuse to play with girls. Sometimes boys and girls can become mortal enemies at this age.

Your son's purposes in joinng various groups and his memberships in them are often of short duration and change frequently, but he will want to be a part of some group. He will want to be like the others, talk like them, and look like them: this is the age of conforming. The gang provides your boy with a certain sense of security and identity. It provides him with a limited means of autonomy from the adult world, where the adults make the rules. He can also learn the value of cooperation through a group. Some gangs can be detrimental, particularly if they encourage delinquent behavior. The boys in the group tend to exclude boys who do not match up to their standards. If a boy is too fat, too short, or too skinny, or if he is from another racial or ethnic background, he may be harshly excluded. Your boy often needs help in accepting others.

Your son will want to emulate those whom he admires. He needs and wants patterns to imitate. He is setting up a picture of what a person should be and identifying himself with that ideal. He will have certain heroes and will want to be like them. His heroes come from books, movies, television, and real life. He dreams about the things he will do and places he will go with his heroes. Those heroes may or may not display behavior that is acceptable in your eyes. It is important that you be aware of whom your son truly admires.

Your son has his primary codes of conduct and justice established by age nine. He understands reasons for most rules and the moral law of cause and effect. You will see him display his extreme concern for the carrying out of proper rules when he is playing games. He will demand justice for his team if it has been wronged. Occasionally he will stand up for what is right according to his convictions, even if it means rejection from his group. He understands truth and honesty and the property and personal rights of others. He likes and needs time for his private thoughts and space for his own things.

Money is becoming more important and useful to your boy. He understands its purpose and the simpler aspects of its use. He does have some conception of saving. He will seek opportunities to earn small sums of money for a goal he has in mind. He appreciates being paid for extra chores around the house. He can understand to a degree some of the financial burdens on the entire family and will appreciate sharing in those concerns. He can assume certain responsibilities related to money matters.

WHAT YOU SHOULD DO

Most of the time your son will not need your help in getting or choosing friends. He can do that well enough on his own. You can help by making sure he will meet other boys his age. He needs neighborhood friends as well as school friends. They may not be the same. Christian friends are valuable. Active participation in church programs will help. If you can get your boy into a Christian Service Brigade Stockade program or AWANA Pals or Pioneers program, you will provide him with plenty of interaction with Christian peers.

If your son has somehow become involved with a bad group of boys, it is best not to promote a holier-than-thou attitude in him. The answer is to seek out Christian families whose children are your son's age and join forces with them in family fun.

This will help your boy develop new friendships that will stabilize during adolescence.

Do not be overly concerned if one of your son's heroes is an undesirable character. If you have provided a solid base of good, character-building values in your home, many of his hero whims will pass. The important thing is to try to expose your boy to as many good adult models as possible. Getting him involved in church and a Stockade or AWANA program will help. Christian camp will also provide good models of adult men.

The proper use of money is an important skill that you should teach your son. You do not want to just hand money to your boy every time he needs or wants it. He should be willing to work and save toward a goal. On the other hand, you do not want to give your son the idea that he gets paid for everything he does around the house. Some things he should be expected to do simply because he is part of the family. The best approach is to assign to your son tasks that he does each day or week. Extra chores that need to be done should be assigned without pay. An allowance of a set amount will give him the pocket money he needs. Some guidelines on how he should or should not spend it are helpful. If your son wants a special item like a baseball glove, you can help him buy it by paying him for a special work project like cleaning out the shed or waxing the car. He will still need your help in these projects, however.

His Intellectual Growth

Your son is broadening his horizons as he grows. He thinks beyond his immediate environment. He has an increasing sense of geography, space, and distance. He may pour over maps, and he will enjoy travel games. He will enjoy having a pen pal from a foreign country if he is encouraged to find one. His historical sense is also developing. He can understand that certain events happened in the past. He can better appreciate stories from the Old Testament, understanding that certain people and places in the past have a relationship to the present. He takes pride in being able to tell time accurately.

The eight-to-eleven-year-old boy is very capable of original ideas and interests, and he is able to put some of his ideas into action. He often makes plans and goes ahead without any adult supervision. Sometimes he will start a project that is too ambitious, or he will just lose interest in a project and drop it without further thought. At this age your boy has accepted most of his parents' values and attitudes about life, but he is beginning to think for himself, to develop his own ideas and points of view. He values other adults' opinions as well as his parents'. He believes most of what his teacher says, but he is coming to realize that even the adults he trusts do not have all the solutions to life's puzzles.

Your son is growing in the breadth of his reading. He talks about what he has read and heard. If your son is not reading by the age of nine, he needs to be carefully examined and given remedial treatment. Some boys this age are great readers; others hardly ever pick up a book. This is the age when difficulties in reading pose a serious problem to his schooling. If he is having trouble reading, he may find it difficult to keep up with his schoolwork, because reading is a part of every assignment in every class. He will feel defeated and discouraged if he cannot read, and he can come to dislike school.

Television can be a powerful influence that expands your son's understanding of life: he learns a great deal about the world around him by watching television. Television can reinforce good examples of appropriate behavior and values. Generosity, self-control, and courage have all been measurably increased in children watching television in test situations. He also gets some distorted viewpoints from television programs. It is estimated that some children spend as much time watching television as they spend in school. Too much time in front of the television can inhibit your child's sense of creativity. It will teach him to be a silent observer rather than an actively involved person.

You may observe that your son is a natural collector of things. His collections now exhibit more organization, purpose, and meaning than they did in his earlier years. In his collecting, value is more important than quantity. He likes to show off his collections.

Your boy still engages in dramatic play. This is an important part of his learning. He will often imitate his favorite heroes or television characters. He can more intelligently act out specific parts.

HOW TO STIMULATE HIS MIND

Your boy at this age is a great discusser. He will find your opinions valuable and will want to compare them with his own opinions, as well as with those of other adults. Be ready to talk with your boy. Sometimes you can stimulate his thinking by asking questions. Become involved with your son in all sorts of activities. Take him places with you. Family excursions are especially valuable. Talk about people and events. This is all part of your ongoing companionship with your son. If he knows that you will listen when he wants to express and discuss an opinion, you will do much to further his intellectual growth.

You can help your son enjoy reading. Help him build his own library of good books on his level. He especially loves books that are filled with adventure, action, and humor. Be sure that he is exposed to a wide range of reading in your home. Bible stories, science fiction, biographical, and fictional materials are all good. Comic books may also be a part of his reading habits. That is all right as long as the comics have acceptable subject matter. Fleming H. Revell Company publishes some comics with Christian themes. If you can afford it, invest in a children's encyclopedia. Help your son learn to use it. You can teach him to find answers to his questions. He should learn

119

to respect these books. Your local library will know the dealers in your area. Purchase your son a subscription to Christian Service Brigade's *Dash* or some other Christian magazine for children. Read the magazine yourself. It will give you a better feel for the interests of your son. A family subscription to *National Geographic* magazine will also interest your son. He will be fascinated by the color photography.

If you have not already done so, set some standards for controlling the kind and number of television programs your son watches. Search out good programs for family viewing. Encourage discussion about what he is watching. Avoid programs with too much violence. Violent shows can cause fears, anxieties, and nightmares for your boy. Also avoid shows that promote open acceptance of promiscuous sex. Those shows tend to confuse and distort your son's sexual understanding. Before you and your son sit down to watch television, ask yourself, "Is there a better way we can spend our time?" You and your wife should try to offer interesting and creative activities as alternatives to most television programs.

HIS SEXUAL UNDERSTANDING

Your son is still interested in sex and what it all means, but his interest between ages ten and eleven is less intense than it was earlier and will be later. His questions are fewer, but he still wants to know the facts. By ten or eleven, if your son has not received adequate instruction, he may be apprehensive about what the facts really are. When your son reaches his eleventh birthday, you would be wise to talk to him about what will happen when he reaches puberty. If your son can anticipate the changes, he will learn to feel much more secure about what is happening to his body.

Modesty becomes important to your boy. He naturally wants to keep himself covered, and he is not really as interested in bare bodies and genitals as he was earlier. He needs privacy in his home and does not like to be interfered with while in the bathroom. He wants you to respect his need for privacy, just as you want him to respect yours.

Your eleven-year-old boy should be prepared to expect occasional emission of semen, sometimes called a wet dream. He should understand that this, like the erection, is a natural occurrence and is nature's way of taking care of sexual activity until he is mature enough to be married.

Your son needs matter-of-fact answers to his questions. Answers still do not need to be detailed. He will ask questions like: Where was I before I was born? How does a baby get outside of the mother? Are fathers necessary for babies to be made? His questions and your answer will depend much on what you have been telling him since his earlier years. The keys to giving him adequate answers are openness, honesty, and getting to the point rather than being evasive.

WHAT HE CAN LEARN SPIRITUALLY

Your son should be able to recognize sin as sin when he hears stories of people doing wrong, but to identify many of his own sins is not so easy. However, your boy will naturally have a keen sense of justice. This will help him feel more responsible for his own wrongdoings. He finds it easier than when younger to understand that God must punish sin, that Jesus took that punishment, and that he needs to give his life to the Lord.

Because your son can now read, he will take a new interest in the Bible if you have encouraged him. Be sure that he has a Bible of his own. A modern version with pictures and maps in it is best. When your son is around ten years old, he can learn to cultivate a daily habit of personal Bible reading. He will learn to do this much more easily if he knows you do it. He also loves to be read to. He particularly loves Bible stories that have plenty of action and heroes. However, he may be bored with stories if he has heard them many times. He will enjoy acting out those stories if encouraged. Your boy can know in a deeper sense that the Bible is God's Word, that it is without error, that it is to be obeyed, and that it provides direct answers for many of the problems he faces in life. But he needs to be guided in finding those answers. Your son can memorize Scripture easily, but his memorizing of verses should be accompanied by explanations from you of the meanings of the Word's truths as they relate to his experiences.

Your son's sense of loyalty can be directed toward church and the Lord. Jesus can also be a kind of hero figure in your son's eyes. A personal relationship with Jesus is generally easy for an eight to eleven year old. He can learn that he needs Jesus Christ to control his life, and that He will help him with his fears. As a result of your example, he will either learn or not learn much of this.

TWELVE

Your Son from Twelve to Fourteen Years Old

His Physical Growth

At around the age of twelve, your son will experience a spurt of growth. The most noticeable change is that his arms and legs will grow longer, and his hands and feet will get bigger. This growth contributes to his apparent clumsiness. Girls will often be taller than boys at this age, and this may make your son feel very self-conscious. Your son's muscles continue to develop. His shoulders and chest broaden, but his growth is uneven and he may feel awkward. Although many consider this to be the clumsy stage, most boys are quite coordinated in many physical activities. There have been tests conducted that show that physical strength, motor abilities, and coordination increase during adolescence. There seems to be a contradiction between an adolescent boy's increased motor coordination and his awkwardness. Your son may be a graceful swimmer, but he will constantly be tripping over his feet; this is the age of contradictions.

During the age of rapid growth, your son has increased nutritional needs. His requirements for minerals and calories are greater. His appetite will increase. You may wonder if he can ever eat enough. He may tire easily and at times appear to be lazy.

Along with his accelerated growth, your son's sex organs begin to mature. He notices with pride that both his penis and scrotum increase in size. Sexual hormones from his testes are

"Well, at least now I won't have to fix the garbage disposal."

also being released, and his secondary sex characteristics begin to appear. Pubic hairs begin to grow. He is able to produce sperm and ejaculate. However, mature sperm cells probably will not develop to any great degree until he is about fifteen. His voice gradually begins to deepen. Sometimes it sounds baritone; other times it sounds soprano. Midway through adolescence, your son may develop slightly enlarged breasts. That is a normal reaction to hormones and it is temporary, but your son can be embarrassed and threatened about this development. He wonders if there is something wrong with his masculinity.

This is the age of acne. That is partly due to eating habits, partly due to emotion, but mostly due to hormone secretions in the body. Depending on the seriousness of the acne your son has, it has the potential of causing him great anxiety about his appearance.

WHAT YOU SHOULD DO

Your son needs your assurance that he is perfectly normal. If he thinks he is too short, assure him that he has got some growing to do yet. If he is sure he is too tall, assure him that many of his friends will catch up sooner or later. Do not make fun of him or ridicule him for his clumsiness. Let him know that you love and accept him the way he is. He will grow out of the awkward stage, and it will not be too long before he will be more physically proficient in some things than you are.

See that your son gets plenty of good food to eat. "Junk food" will not kill him and may even help satisfy his increased caloric needs. Of course, too much "junk food" is not good either, and how much of it he eats should be controlled. Do not make your son think he is a pig. He is extremely self-conscious and needs your words of acceptance. If your son has problems with obesity, you will do him a great service by not being critical of his fatness. Many boys' chubbiness rounds out in later adolescence. If he really does need to lose weight, give him the emotional support he needs to diet. Seek medical advice on how he should go about dieting.

Be aware of your son's physical sexual changes. You can relieve much of his apprehension about those changes by talking to him about them. The most important thing you can do, however, is to not make fun of his squeaky voice, his desire to grow a beard, or his concerns about the size of his genitals. Those are extremely important things to him. If you make fun of him, you may lose much of his confidence in you to discuss his anxieties about his physical changes.

His Emotional Development

Much of your son's self-image during this age is related to his physical growth. His feelings about himself are rooted there. He can become very moody. He can be up and down emotionally within the same hour. He can be withdrawn and daydream during a family get-together. At other times he will be brash and argumentative, or friendly and laughing.

He needs his own sense of self-identity, but his body, emotions, and thinking often confuse him. He is trying to find out who he is. He seeks much more independence than he did when he was younger. He still needs and wants his parents' guidance, love, and support. He does not generally feel good about himself. He thinks he is either too short, too tall, or too fat. He thinks he is not growing as he should. In the locker room, he may wonder why his penis is not as large as the penises of some other boys, or why he does not yet have pubic hairs. He may be a perfectly handsome young man to you, but he will probably think his ears, his nose, or some other parts of his body are ugly.

Your son is striving to be treated like and considered an adult, and indeed, much of his behavior is more mature than his youthful looks would lead you to expect. However, your son is basically immature. He can be very childish at times— temperamental, selfish, and irresponsible. He is in a transition

126

from childhood to adulthood, and this transition can be a frustrating and confusing experience for him and for you, his parents.

WHAT YOU SHOULD DO

Much of your son's emotional state is related to your attitudes about him. Not all boys will rebel or ignore their father's advice. You can maintain a meaningful and helpful relationship with your son. Do not take your son's negative attitudes and withdrawal as a personal attack. If you approach your son with a positive rather than a negative attitude, many of his emotional insecurities can be ironed out. If you find that you cannot communicate with your boy, read chapter 21 to get some helpful suggestions.

Remember that you cannot give your son everything he needs. He needs and wants to step out on his own and learn for himself. Sometimes it will take courage on your part, but you need to give him opportunities to be responsible in spite of his immaturity. He will fail at times, but he will also succeed. Stand behind him in his failures to act responsibly. This does not mean you are to ignore his irresponsibility. He needs firm discipline, but he needs to be built up, not belittled.

Help your son see that there is much more to becoming a worthwhile person than having good looks. Talk to him about your feelings when you were a teenager and how you overcame some of your anxieties. Try not to laugh at him when he expresses his emotional difficulties. His feelings can be easily hurt, although he may not show it. Give him constructive help and friendly reassurance.

How He Gets Along with Others

Your son's peer group has a much more profound influence on him at this age than it did when he was younger. Belonging to a group often reassures the adolescent boy of his personal worth. If he is rejected by his peers, it will cause some deep hurts. He uses his friends to support him. On the other hand, peer pressure will often cause your boy to try to be something he really is not so that he can be like his friends. He will look to his peers as a reference for many values and decisions, but that does not indicate a total rejection of his parents' values. Studies show that if your son is relatively well adjusted, he has adopted your values, and the influences his peers exert will pass with time.

Peer pressure may cause your child to experiment with smoking, drugs, and alcohol. There is a big difference between experimentation and abuse of these vices. So if you discover some experimentation, do not be shocked or overreact. If your son is reasonably emotionally secure, the experimentation will pass. On the other hand, if your son is heavily involved with drugs and alcohol, it is usually because he is emotionally unstable and may not have a healthy relationship with you. For some helpful suggestions, read chapter 21. It may also be advisable to seek clinical help.

As your son matures, he will turn from his self-questioning and self-centered ways and develop a real interest in other people. He can reach out to others in genuine love. He has leadership capacities, but he still needs adult guidance.

Most boys this age like girls, but probably are not emotionally mature enough to begin dating. There is usually a maturity difference of about two years between boys and girls until ages fifteen and sixteen when boys begin to catch up. Your son will lack self-confidence unless he is especially handsome and athletic. But even if he is so endowed, he may not have enough interest in dating to try it.

Your son enjoys physical activity and competition with other males. He enjoys being with adult men who provide him with different models. Participation in a Christian Service Brigade's Battalion or Task Force program, an AWANA program, or a denominational youth program will do much to help him develop socially.

128

Your boy at this age may be very critical of you, his parents, mostly about things of little significance. You may not measure up to some of his standards! He often compares you and your wife with the parents of his friends, and he wonders why you do not do things the way they do. However, if your son is being raised in a generally happy atmosphere, he is proud of his mom and dad deep inside, and his petty criticisms will pass with time.

WHAT YOU SHOULD DO

You need to realize the importance of your son's peers. At this point in his life he may need to conform to his friends' ways of thinking in order to grow emotionally and socially. Dogmatically forcing him to conform to your values will do more harm than good at this point. If you discover that his friends have influenced him to try drugs, alcohol, or tobacco, you need to confront him, not in a judgmental way, but in an understanding way, encouraging him to talk about why he tried the particular substance. Be honest and open with him. Let him know your feelings about those things. Discourage his use of those things, but realize that sometimes he may experiment to learn for himself.

Encourage your boy to join a Christian Service Brigade Battalion or Task Force program or an AWANA Pioneers program, if there is one near you. These programs are designed with your boy's specific interests in mind. They encourage him to socialize with other Christian boys and men, without the pressures he feels in a coeducational group. These programs also help develop his leadership skills and prepare him to be a Christian man of the future. The spiritual emphasis of the programs will also be beneficial to him.

You or your wife should not pressure your son to begin dating in this age period. He will date in his own time. You can be sure that he has opportunity to mingle occasionally with girls his own age other than in school. Church youth activities are the natural place to start.

As far as your boy's critical nature is concerned, patience is the best approach. He does need to maintain an attitude of respect toward you and his mother. And overdone and vicious criticism should not be allowed. But you need to be on guard against a more common problem than sons being overly critical of their parents. The more common problem is that parents, especially fathers, are too critical of their sons. Almost everything their sons do or do not do fails to meet their expectations. They are constantly "disappointed" in their boys. What it boils down to is that nine times out of ten, fathers expect too much of their sons. A conscious effort to be patient, to refrain from nagging and criticizing will do much to help your son mature. A positive, supportive attitude on your part is what your son needs and probably does not get enough of. Granted, it takes much to be positive toward a young teen. This is a test of your own maturity.

His Intellectual Growth

Along with your son's physical growth spurt comes a new surge in intellectual growth. His ability to reason is much improved: he can think through complex problems much easier than he could when he was younger. He is introspective and a deep thinker, and he has formulated many ideas and beliefs from his own thinking. He can think abstractly, and he now understands symbolism. This ability to think symbolically will give him a much greater comprehension of life. Because of increased knowledge and better means of communication, your son is bombarded with much more information about life than you were when you were a child. It is often difficult for him to assimilate all this information.

He is an idealist, and this will greatly influence his perspective on relationships with family, friends, church, community, and world. His idealism is genuine, and it will give him the motivation he needs to be innovative and creative.

Your son has a much-increased capacity to think about and plan for the future. He can reason about far-reaching consequences. This may make him wonder and worry about the future world—and what it will be like and how he will fit into it. He may or may not be interested in thoughts about a career. Interest in a career at this age varies with each boy, and your boy still has plenty of time to think about his choice of a career.

Your son is capable of purely academic pursuits, but he enjoys learning by doing. He is action oriented. He gets on certain "kicks" such as sports, collecting cans, reading science fiction and thrilling adventures, and cars.

Your son can be an avid reader, although this will only be true if you have cultivated his interest in books through his childhood. He will enjoy reading humorous stories, fiction with suspense and action, science and science fiction, and true stories about famous people. He will also enjoy reading humorous magazines, the selection of which you should supervise.

Because of the many emotional changes your son is experiencing during these years, his schoolwork may deteriorate. Grades may be somewhat lower than they were in elementary school. However, the junior high school curriculum offers students a wide selection of courses to choose from to suit their interests, and many boys do well because they are in classes they like.

HOW TO STIMULATE HIS MIND

Try not to downplay your son's idealism. Offer your experienced perspective when he is expressing his own ideas, but do your best to encourage his ideas rather than squelch them. Believe in your son. Believe that he can be motivated enough to do things he believes in. Help him in any way you can. He needs you to be optimistic about life and its struggles.

Your son may want to talk to you about various careers. He may or may not develop interest in your career field. You may want him to do better in life than you have. Pressuring him to go to college, however, can be a mistake. You certainly have the right to express your feelings about what you would like to see him do, but you will do your son a much greater service if you expose him to various possibilities and let *him* choose. Now may or may not be a good time for him to develop interests that are career related. Whatever you do, do not rush him into considering a career. He has enough to worry about in terms of his body, emotions, and relationships.

Encourage your son in good reading material. Know what he is reading and what his interests are. Purchase him a subscription to Christian Service Brigade's *Venture* magazine, *Campus Life* magazine, or *Young Ambassador* magazine. A family set of encyclopedia and a subscription to *National Geographic* will help him in his educational pursuits. A news magazine like *Time, Newsweek,* or *U.S. News and World Report* is also good to have around to support his interest in current events.

Be aware of and show interest in your son's schooling. Encourage but do not pressure him toward high grades. Pressuring him will cause him considerable anxiety. Accept your son at his own level of academic ability. If your boy is consistently doing poorly in school, it is probably because he is experiencing some deep emotional insecurities. You may want to seek advice from his teachers and the school principal. For some further suggestions on encouraging your son in schooling and achievement, see chapter 18.

What He Can Learn Spiritually

Because your son can grasp abstract concepts, he now can learn deep spiritual truths. He can begin to grasp the concept of the Trinity. He can have a much deeper understanding than before of what salvation means because the concepts behind redemption, the sin nature, and how Jesus bore our sins on the cross are all much clearer to him. It would be wise to discuss these subjects with your son to see how much he understands. You can help him a great deal by clarifying certain things he may be confused about.

Your son can have a much better understanding of what the Body of Christ is all about. He can know what spiritual gifts are, although he will have difficulty identifying his own. If he has committed himself to Christ, he should be able to become a member of your church. He can understand the meaning of Communion, and after instruction he should be allowed to partake. His participation in a church depends a great deal on your own involvement. If you are involved, he will be also; if you are not, he probably won't be, either.

Your son will probably want to be involved in church. If he is a member, he will want to think that he is a vital part of the body. He has the capacity to know and experience what it means to serve others. He wants and needs guided opportunities in leadership. Remember that your son is one of the future leaders of the church. Active participation in a well-planned youth program will help. Again, being part of a Christian Service Brigade Battalion or Task Force program or an AWANA Pioneers program will give him the guidance and opportunities he needs for Christian service and leadership. He will also be exposed to Christian men who are different from yourself. That exposure is excellent for developing your son into a Christian man.

Your son is developing some definite Christian values of his own, but he is seeking answers to many questions he has about morals, ethics, and spirituality. He is beginning to question and may openly reject some of your Christian values. Deep inside he wants to do what is right and submit to God's authority, but he is searching for answers he can call his own. He will

133

particularly question imposed guidelines set by his parents and church that have been made absolute. He is very perceptive and can identify hypocrisies and double standards.

This questioning and searching in the son's Christian faith is difficult for many Christian fathers to face. You may see your boy swaying in his faith. Feeling protective, you may find yourself arguing with your son and forcing on him what you believe is right. Your best approach is to encourage your son to discuss his questions with you. Be open with him, however; express your feelings and beliefs, but allow him to disagree with you. Force yourself to take the risk of treating him as an equal. Do not belittle him or think you must put him in his place. Realize that his searching and questioning approach is a healthy way for him to come to terms with spiritual matters on his own. In the end, he will be a much better Christian for it.

His Sexual Understanding

Your son has a new interest in sex when he reaches the age of twelve. He is becoming a sexual being, and that has profound effects on his emotions and social relationships. Your son may know about the hormone changes in his body, but he may not understand why he "feels" different. He is extremely self-conscious about his changing body, and he may wonder if he is normal.

Your son experiences vivid sexual fantasies and wonders if something is wrong with him. He wonders why he has such a preoccupation with sex. Masturbation will probably increase, along with subsequent guilt feelings. A Christian young man has the same fantasies and sexual feelings that a non-Christian has. He cannot deny his feelings, but he wants to know what is right behavior.

In his search for sexual identity, your son will often confuse love and sex. From the media and school he is bombarded with a confused concept of sexuality. The heavy emphasis on "making love" in our society is misleading and detrimental to a young person's developing the proper emotional maturity necessary for marriage and love between a man and a woman. The biblical guidelines are clear, but they are constantly being distorted, challenged and ridiculed. Witnessing a healthy, loving relationship between you and your wife will help your son get the proper perspective.

The key to helping your son in his new sexuality is keeping the line of communication open between the two of you. His emergence into a sexual person can be frightening, but ignoring the subject will do more harm than good. Be sympathetic toward his sexual conflicts. Keeping him well informed and letting him know what you think is proper sexual behavior will do much toward his becoming a mature adult. Be sure to emphasize consistently the biblical guidelines.

"Nice to meet you, Marsha. Now we know why Junior has
been changing his socks every day."

THIRTEEN

Your Son from Fifteen to Eighteen Years Old

Your son at ages fifteen to eighteen is emerging from early adolescence (ages twelve to fourteen). To get a more complete perspective on your boy's overall development, you should read this chapter and the chapter titled "Your Son from Twelve to Fourteen Years Old." Because there are so many similarities between these two age groups, we will not go into as much detail in this chapter as we did in the previous chapter. However, there are some sharp differences between boys in the two age groups, and they are important to know in understanding your son's further development.

His Physical Growth

Your boy at this age has nearly completed the physical changes he was going through from ages twelve to fourteen. His muscles are more defined. He will probably grow a little taller. Most boys are taller than girls at this age. His body proportions have stabilized, and his former awkwardness is passing. Soon he will begin to show signs of a beard, and he will probably need to start shaving once or twice a week. This is an important time for your son, and he should not be teased about it. Soon he will have the body of an adult, and he will generally feel pretty good about it. However, some boys develop slowly. The size of his penis may not have changed much. He may not have any pubic hair. He may wonder if he will ever grow up. If your boy is a slow developer, you must realize that this is not abnormal. He will be very apprehensive about his slow development, and he will often be ridiculed by his peers. Any joking about it on your part will be taken as an insult. He needs your sympathetic encouragement to be patient. He will "arrive" sooner or later.

His Emotional Development

Your son's emotions are probably much more in balance now than they were earlier. His moodiness has calmed, and he has a more even disposition. His feelings are still strong, and some of the hurts he received as an early teen may still be bothering him, but he will repress them more. He has a growing need to be more independent. He finds value in a part-time job or even full-time work during the summer months. At fifteen or sixteen he will want to get his driver's license. The job and driver's license are symbols of adulthood to him. They give him the freedom he needs. He sees himself as grown up and finds it increasingly difficult to submit to your restrictions. If you are going to maintain a helpful relationship with your son, you need to allow him to express himself. Be patient as he strives to be "his own man." Repressing his efforts to do so will lead to a decisive break between you and him.

How He Gets Along with Others

Your son still confides in his group of friends, although he may have enough self-confidence to begin to shake off some of the influence of the group. He is becoming more of an individual, making judgments and holding opinions that are his own and not the group's. But for the most part he still looks to his friends for advice. In general, friendships are deeper and more mature than they were earlier.

His interest in girls is increasing and he should feel more secure in handling himself around them. He will want to begin dating, and he will need you to set some guidelines.

Your son's first dating experience may be very exciting to him. He will probably be nervous and somewhat unsure of himself. He may be too shy to talk about his feelings with you. He may appreciate some words of encouragement from you. It is important that you do not tease him about this first experience, because it is not a light matter with him.

There is no "right" age for dating to start as far as teenage boys are concerned. It depends too much on the individual boy. More importantly, it is very dangerous to force dating on your son. If he is not ready emotionally, no matter what his age, he will resent being pushed into it. On the other hand, if your son is ready, he needs your encouragement. You need to be sensitive to how he is reacting to girls. Talking to him about how he feels will help you determine if he is ready . Even before your boy is ready for his first date, it is important for you to set some clear guidelines. Those guidelines will cover times, places he can or cannot go, how to treat a girl with respect, money, use of the car, and dating alone versus dating with another couple. Double dating may be the best way for your boy to start.

There is much debate over the issue of "going steady." Committing himself to one girl limits your son's flexibility in socializing. Our feeling is that going steady should be discouraged in the early teen years. On the other hand, your boy may know only one girl who is willing to date him, and he may wish to date her several times in a row before dating another girl. When your son reaches seventeen or eighteen, if he wants to go steady in the true sense of committing himself to one girl he especially likes, you probably should allow him to do so. At that age, he should be more mature in choosing such a relationship. If he is not going to college, he may be more serious about finding the right mate for marriage, and engagement may follow, but he should be aware of the potential hurts involved in the more serious arrangement. You should be open with him and express your feelings about marriage right out of high school, but if he is really emotionally attached to one girl, he will need to decide for himself.

You are probably wondering if you should regulate whom your son dates. You will not want your son to date just any girl, but it is almost impossible to scrutinize all his friends. The best way to encourage your son to date wholesome girls is to begin when he is young and instill in him high standards of personal conduct. Encouraging him in the youth activities of your church will help keep him in contact with the kinds of Christian girls you want him to date. Also encourage him to bring his friends home, both male and female. This alone will do much toward helping him judge good relationships.

His Intellectual Growth

The biggest intellectual concern for your son at this age is his future career. He faces many alternatives in today's world. If he wants to go to college, he needs to choose where to go. He needs to choose a direction of study. His grades have to be good. These are all major concerns for your boy, and he will need your advice. There are two important things you can do for your boy in his efforts to choose a career. The first and most important is to *talk with him about it*. At times your son may not act like it, but your opinions and advice are important to him. The second thing is to not go overboard and force your son to go in the direction you want him to go. Do not be fooled by the misconception that "in order to get anyplace in this world, you have to go to college." That may have been true twenty-five years ago, but it is not so today. There are hundreds of valuable vocations your son can get into without a college degree. Vocational schools enjoy increasing attendance, and the graduates of those schools are going into meaningful and well-paying occupations.

When your son reaches his junior year in high school, he will need to make some decision about the direction of his future.

If he plans to go to college or vocational school, he should apply early in his senior year. To prepare for his future occupation, he will need help in formulating his curriculum for his junior and senior years. A school guidance counselor will help, but again, you can and should be involved in giving your son direction. To do this effectively, you should be aware of the curricular options available to him.

HIS SEXUAL UNDERSTANDING

By now your son has all the basic facts and more about sex. His feelings and confusions about sex are not as intense as they were earlier. He has much better control of his feelings, but he is still very interested in sexual things. He is generally more mature about sexual matters, and he can talk about them more freely without being overly embarrassed, even in mixed groups. He is still bombarded with distortions about love and sex. Premarital sex is common in public schools. It is much more accepted and open than in junior high school and your son may be considered "square" if he has not participated in promiscuous sex. Your son may have high standards on how to treat a girl, but his temptations are no less intense than anyone else's, especially if he is dating a "willing" girl. He may experience some kissing and petting in his dating, and he may carry some guilt. You may be surprised by how much he will tell you if you have kept the communication lines open all along and he knows he can talk openly with you without fear of condemnation.

WHAT HE CAN LEARN SPIRITUALLY

Your son's experience and ability to do more sophisticated thinking at ages fifteen to eighteen enable him to think in deeper and more serious terms about spiritual things. He is still searching for his own answers about life and his relationship to God. Your boy may develop a special interest in some of the more complicated theological issues as boys often do. If this is true of your boy, you can help him a great deal by encourag-

141

ing his spiritual interests. Discuss his questions with him. Give him your insights and opinions, but avoid arguing with him. You can challenge his thoughts, but show respect for his opinions, too.

If your son has been involved in church up to this point, he may have a growing interest in being a vital part of the church. As was stated earlier, he thinks he is grown up and appreciates being treated that way. He is willing to take on more responsibility, and if encouraged he will appreciate opportunities to serve and lead. A wise church will do all it can to present older teens with such meaningful opportunities.

There are also many fine opportunities for Christian service available to your son through service-oriented organizations like Teen Missions. Other missionary organizations and camps offer short-term service opportunities. You will do well to encourage your son to get involved in these.

Obviously, not all boys are interested in church activities. In his search for himself, your son may rebel against his parents and the church he grew up in. There are many reasons for this, and we do not have the space here to discuss them. If your boy has rejected you and the church, it is important that you seek to maintain an understanding relationship with him. This is vital. Beyond seeking the Lord in prayer and depending on the Holy Spirit to work in your son's life, you can do little else. You do not necessarily need to blame yourself for his rejection. Your son is responsible for his own relationship to God. If you have provided him with a relatively secure family life, he may very well come back into the fold.

PART 3

LEARN TO DO YOUR JOB BETTER

"It hurts more than he said it would."

FOURTEEN

How to Discipline Your Son

What can we say about discipline that has not been said already many times? Although there is nothing entirely new to be said, in this chapter we want to focus on some concerns that young fathers may have. We will examine those concerns using a question-and-answer format.

How can I be sure I am disciplining my son in the right way?

We take this question first because it influences the following questions. There is no *one* right way. The more you read and hear about discipline (even from evangelical Christians), the more you realize that there is a variety of approaches at your disposal. What is important is to apply the best of those approaches to the needs of your son. Each child is different and requires discipline suited to him. This means that you and your wife must develop your own strategy for each child. Take the best from each approach and fit it into your goals in disciplining.

My wife and I do not agree on disciplining procedures. She thinks I am too lenient. What should we do?

At the very least, keep your disagreements between the two of you. Support each other in front of your children; otherwise, they will play you against their mother. What you must do is develop a joint strategy for disciplining. A strategy is a plan of action. In formulating this plan, consider the following questions.

- What are the goals of our disciplining?
- What acts of disobedience warrant physical spanking, if any?
- What other methods of disciplining will we use, and when?
- What daily actions will we take to encourage obedience?
- What specific actions in disciplining will we avoid?

Many of your disagreements can be ironed out through this planning. A disciplining strategy should be reviewed about once a year. Changes should be made to accommodate the growing maturity of your children.

What should our goals be in disciplining?

Here you will discover a great variety of suggestions from a variety of sources. You may be able to accept most of them, or you may choose only one or two.

A popular goal is to build self-discipline in your children. One writer calls self-discipline being self-motivated to behave in socially desirable ways. When your son is able to behave maturely and independently, you can consider this goal achieved.

Another well-known goal is to develop respect for authority. If your son learns to obey you, he will then be able to obey the authorities in society. In this way, he will be a responsible member of society.

The Bible adds another dimension. Discipline must produce righteousness and holiness (Hebrews 12:5-11). The goal of all Christians is to become Christlike in character (Ephesians 4:13). Through the family, a Christian's nature (father, mother, or child) is shaped by God. This goal of Christlikeness is difficult to grasp, but it focuses on building character, and not just on dealing with misbehavior. It shows the positive side of discipline.

146

How can I avoid being too harsh with my son? I do not want him to hate me.

If you are a father who maintains strict discipline in your home, you are in the minority. According to a noted authority on fathers, Henry Biller, more than half the fathers in the country are not involved in setting limits. If you are in the minority, you have chosen the better direction. Actually, you do not have to worry about being too strict if you are normally warm and affectionate toward your son and especially affectionate after you have disciplined him. Your son will respect your firm hand if he knows you love him.

Your son will know you love him, not because you tell him, but because you show him. Physical affection and a good dose of personal attention, using plenty of warm eye contact, are two ways to show love. Verbal expressions serve as reinforcement to your actions. Let your son know that your love for him will always be there no matter what he does. When you must apply some form of discipline, continue your affectionate caring. You should actually view disciplining as another way to show love.

When should I start spanking (if at all), and when should I stop?

Spanking is one method of discipline. Reference is made to some form of physical discipline in Proverbs, although the "rod" spoken of in those passages was a heavy instrument not at all suited for use on small children. "Beating with a rod" was for older persons, much like a public scourging. Obviously, small children are not subjects for that kind of discipline.

Spanking using the hand or a paddle on your boy's hand or backside *can* be used during his early years (ages one to three) as a conditioning mechanism. The experience of pain helps a child avoid certain actions.

This is useful only because you cannot talk with your child and explain why he should not do something you have forbidden him to do. But often there are other ways to handle a situ-

147

ation (e.g., remove a temptation) that avoid spanking. Use them first. As a general rule, avoid excessive spanking in the very early years (ages one to three). Try to avoid confrontations, and use spankings as a conditioning technique only as a last resort.

Remember that our twentieth-century culture creates many of the problems that a child experiences during these early years. As Gene Getz said in *The Measure of a Family* (Glendale, Calif.: Regal, 1976),

> Think how few problems children (and parents) have growing up in a society where there are no intriguing television dials to turn, no inviting electrical outlets on the wall, no colorful knobs on gas and electric stoves, no kitchen cupboards with handles at eye-level, filled with noisy equipment that appeals to the inner cravings of a two-year-old. . . . We must face the fact that our twentieth-century Western culture has complicated life for both parents and children. And the children are the ones who must conform. In many instances, this is the root of a lot of problems in child-rearing, as well as behavioral problems in later life (pp. 110-11).

When your boy is past the age of three, physical spankings should be reserved for serious situations (e.g., when he directly defies a parent's authority) and used only in the context of a loving discussion. Make sure you understand your child's perspective of a misdeed.

The indiscriminate use of spankings can build resentment or fear in your son. This is particularly true when he is very young, because small children tend to repress their feelings because of fear of pain. Utilize other methods, and keep spanking as the last resort, whatever your boy's age. This is easier said than done, but careful planning of your disciplining strategy will serve you well in the "heat of the battle."

As your child approaches the teenage years, spankings should cease, and other methods should be used that respect a boy's older age and sense of responsibility.

Should I as the father assume the role of disciplinarian in my home?

If you mean that only you discipline and not your wife, the answer is *no*. Marriage is an equal partnership when it comes to disciplining your son. You are responsible to take leadership, but you will need your wife's involvement very much. It is important that you back up and respect your wife's authority.

When I sit down with my son to discipline my son, what do I do?

There are several things to keep in mind. Do this privately— only you and your son. Spend a few minutes listening to him. Try to understand his side of the issue. Encourage him to express his feelings. Let him know that you love him and accept him, but that you must do something about his disobedient actions. God requires this of you. Apply the relevant discipline (e.g., a spanking, a restriction), and then be warm and tender to him. When this session is over, consider the case closed.

I dislike coming home from work and immediately having to discipline my boy for things he has done during the day. How do I get away from that?

You have reason to dislike this role. It makes you seem like an ogre and instills fear of you in your son ("Wait until Daddy comes home. He'll get you!"). Your wife should take care of most problems during the day. More serious problems that require your attention should be handled in the evening when the time is right (usually after dinner). As the father who has been away most of the day, you can provide an objective perspective on a problem. It is important that you get involved.

What are my choices when it comes to methods of discipline?

You have a variety of options. You can reinforce good behavior by rewards and praise. You can let the child experience the natural consequences of his actions (e.g., sleeping in and

149

being late for school). With teenagers, you indicate your approval or disapproval through discussion. Certain restrictions can be placed on a boy for certain misbehaviors (e.g., no television for not coming home on time). Restrictions, or depriving your child of some pleasure, are always better than making your child do some kind of work as punishment. The latter breeds bad attitudes toward work. Physical spanking should be employed for severe cases, especially outright rebellion against parental authority. Generally, physical spanking begins after the boy's first year and lasts until he reaches puberty.

Should I bring the Bible into discipline? If so, how?

Yes, use the Bible, but not as a club. Letting your children know that the Bible tells parents to train their children in the way of the Lord is very good. You are under obligation to God's standards for parents. In doing this, you set an example of obedience yourself. Your family devotional time could include a study of some of the passages that deal with parental responsibility: Hebrews 12:5-11; Ephesians 6:1-4; Proverbs 13:24; 22:15; 23:13-14; 29:15, 17. The entire book of Proverbs is great for learning God's guidelines for family living.

Why is discipline such a major issue?

Most parents sense they need help in this area. Much confusion can be eliminated by understanding the word "discipline" more fully. It means more than punishment, which is simply the consequence of wrongdoing, or disobedience. Discipline is also a positive activity in which you provide direction and guidance to your child. You are establishing patterns of responsible living in your son that will prevent situations in which you must punish. When you discipline this way, trying to develop self-discipline in your son, you give your child challenging projects, like jobs to do around the house. Discipline does not make life easy for children, but it builds character.

150

Can you give me a foolproof, simple formula for disciplining my son?

You are probably thinking, *That's impossible.* You are partly right. But having a handful of principles to keep in mind at all times is helpful. You feel less confused. One author has a list of twelve "don'ts" that includes using threats, being inconsistent, using rules inappropriate for the age of the child, and giving commands you will not enforce. Another boils them down to eight "dos" and "don'ts." Among them are do admit your mistakes and do not make comparisons of one child with another.

We can give you these general principles.

● Cultivate your relationship with God. He will increase your love.

● Work at your relationship with your son. Show your love to him.

● Remember that discipline is a long-range process. You will lose some battles along the way, but you will win (have a disciplined son) in the end if you work at it.

"To learn the sex of a chicken, you can look at the egg and get no hint at all!"

FIFTEEN

How to Influence Your Son's Sexuality

An exciting feature of the job of being father is the built-in influence you have upon your son. You have natural influence that comes with being a father. One area in which this influence can be used to great effect is the sexuality of your boy.

By sexuality we mean your child's understanding of the reproduction process and how his own body functions sexually, his moral standards about sexual activity, his attitudes and feelings about his body, and his ability to act comfortably and responsibly with members of the opposite sex.

Your goals for your son's sexuality are important. They may include some of these: correct knowledge of the human reproduction process; an appreciation for his own body and a desire to use it for God's glory; a commitment to sexual purity and God's plan for sex in marriage; responsible dating habits; and ease in talking to and getting along with girls.

There are numerous practical ways for you to influence your son's sexuality toward these goals. We will suggest five. More information can also be found in chapters 12 and 13.

First, develop an atmosphere of easy conversation about sex. You can make sex a natural and normal topic of discussion in your home, a topic to be discussed without embarrassment or shame. For starters, use the proper names for the body's organs and functions. Treat urination and bowel movements (and changing diapers!) as things to be expected.

When children ask questions about their bodies or about

babies, answer their questions honestly. Children usually are not interested in much detail, but only in the basic idea. Getting answers to questions is the most effective way of learning about sex.

At the same time, maintain a respectful attitude toward sex. If your son comes home with a foul word or a crude joke, let him know why it is inappropriate. Do not make him feel guilty about this, although you should let him know that it will be considered disobedience if he uses the word again. Indicate to him the standards of purity in your home.

Second, let your relationship to your wife be a positive example. Your son will form impressions of marriage and of how men should treat women from observing you in action. If you display affection and respect toward your wife in front of him, you help to show the love that is needed in marriage and sex.

Your daughter's future choice of a husband is deeply influenced by how you treat her and her mother. If she feels close to you and appreciates the way you treat her mother, she is likely to select a mate much like you and enjoy a stable marriage.

All your children will feel comfortable and secure when they know you and your wife are close and intimate with each other (it is pretty hard to hide it if you are not). Marriage then becomes an attractive goal for adult life.

Third, be affectionate with your son at all ages. Many men have great difficulty in this area. Usually, they have not been affectionate with their fathers. Now they are passing the same attitude on to their own sons.

This pattern can be broken if a man decides that touching, hugging, and kissing his child, no matter what the child's age, are normal parts of being a father, just as they are normal acts of a mother. Although boys may rebel against this at certain ages (around nine to fourteen years old), they treasure your tenderness as a sign of acceptance. It is usually almost impossible to harbor ill feelings toward each other when you are holding hands or hugging. Sexual overtones to this kind of affection, whether for sons or daughters, are usually grossly exaggerated and need to be put out of your mind.

You may have to force yourself to be affectionate. But think of the benefits: greater intimacy in your family now and greater ability of your children to be affectionate to their spouses and children in the future.

Fourth, read and discuss biblical passages about sex. It is important that your son recognize that the Bible has much to say about sex in clear, frank terms, as a reading of the Song of Solomon will show. Whenever you talk to your child about his own body or facts about sex, add a word about God's plan. Refer to a Scripture passage if possible. All this helps to show God's interest and provision in our sexuality.

Books for children about sex written by Christians are also helpful in explaining a biblical perspective. Check the resources on page 199 for some suggestions.

You can explore biblical passages with your family on a whole range of topics such as: (1) marriage: Genesis 2:20-25; Matthew 19:3-12; 1 Corinthians 7:3-4; Ephesians 5:22-23; (2) sexual activity: Genesis 39; Exodus 20:14; Leviticus 18:6; Proverbs 5—6; Romans 1:24-25; 1 Thessalonians 4:1-8; Hebrews 13:4; (3) our bodies: Psalm 139:13-15; Romans 6:12-13; Romans 12:1; 1 Corinthians 6:12-20; (4) control of physical desires: Matthew 5:27-32; Galatians 5:19-24; 2 Timothy 2:22; and (5) impure thoughts: Ephesians 5:5; Philippians 4:8.

Fifth, create special teaching opportunities. Although spontaneous questions from your son in the give-and-take of family life are the best opportunities for teaching, you can also take the initiative in teaching him when situations from which he can learn come along.

The conception and birth of another child in your family provide a great setting for instruction. As your wife's uterus expands, you can explain how a baby lives and grows. Dia-

155

grams can help show this. When the baby is born, the birth process can be explained.

As your son approaches puberty, you may wish to make a special occasion for talking to him in detail about adolescence. Author James Dobson recommends that fathers do this with their children around the age of ten or eleven. In particular, explain what physical changes will happen in him, the sexual drive he will have, your expectations for his dating, how sexual intercourse happens, and the pressures he will feel at this time in his life. Assure him that you will love and accept him even when there are conflicts between the two of you.

SIXTEEN

How to Help Your Son's Spiritual Growth

Along with discipline, your son's spiritual development is probably your major concern. This concern usually focuses on such matters as your son's becoming a Christian and showing genuine interest in Christian growth. You are also concerned about taking spiritual leadership in your home through such formal teaching situations as family devotions.

A complicating factor in your role as spiritual leader is that you are dealing with an area that is ultimately out of your control. The spiritual growth of your son is in God's hands. You cannot make the boy grow spiriually. Only the Holy Spirit produces growth. All you can do is fulfill your responsibilities. As in personal witnessing, simply do your part and leave the results to God.

Wanting to do your part well in your son's spiritual growth is a desire that you have in common with most fathers. The following questions explore how you can be a good father in this area.

Exactly what should I be trying to do for my son's spiritual growth? The best way to answer this question is to list some goals you might have:

• He will believe in Jesus Christ as Savior and Lord and have a personal relationship with Him.

• He will know the Bible and submit to its authority.

• He will pray regularly and see God answer prayer.

157

"Dad, what is justification?"

• He will live a holy life of obedience to God's Word, a life that is marked by love and service to others.

• He will tell his friends about Jesus Christ.

• He will become an active member of a local church.

• He will worship and praise God as a routine of life.

To accomplish these goals, you have at least three methods at your disposal. All three of these methods are described in the classic passage to fathers, Deuteronomy 6:4-9.

The first method of encouraging your son's spiritual growth is *personal example*. This is implied in verses 5 and 6, in which men are commanded to love God and have the Word of God planted in their hearts. Fathers who live this way show their sons the way of the Lord in "living color." The second method is some kind of *formal instruction*. This is implied in the first part of verse 7: "You shall teach them diligently to your sons" (NASB).* There are many ways to teach God's Word to your sons, but you, the father, must do it and you must do it with planning and perseverance. The third method, as seen in the last part of verse 7, is *informal teaching:* "When you sit in your house and when you walk by the way and when you lie down and when you rise up" (NASB). All the normal living experiences of the day offer opportunities to teach. You must take advantage of them.

What is a good age for my son to accept Christ? There is no one best age at which your son can accept Christ. It can happen as early as four years of age or as late as your son's adulthood. Many boys make this decision during their junior years (eight to eleven), a time when Christian men can be a great influence on them. Decisions made during the teenage years are usually meaningful and firm commitments.

How can I encourage my son to follow Christ without pressuring him? From the earliest years of his life, make sure your son understands that he must decide to become a Christian. Mention this when you pray with him, but treat it as a decision

New American Standard Bible

159

he will make when he is ready. Wait for him to approach you with the desire to talk about becoming a Christian.

Actually, it does not pay to pressure your son by asking him if he wants to accept Christ now. A person is saved when the Holy Spirit regenerates him, not when you get him to say the right words. Just keep praying for your son and trusting the Holy Spirit to convict your son of his need for salvation.

You will have many opportunities to explain the way of salvation to your son. Do not hesitate to do it, and include a testimony of how Christ has changed your life.

If my son tells me that he wants to be a Christian, what do I say to him? Sit down with him privately and get out your Bible. Go over the steps to salvation in Christ. There are three things that your son must do, regardless of his age. You will have to explain these at a level he can understand.

● *He must believe that he is a sinner.* Read Romans 3:23 in your Bible. If possible, have your son read it. A younger boy will understand his being a sinner in the sense of his having committed specific sins, like disobedience. A teenage boy may be able to grasp the idea of man's sinful nature.

● *He must believe that Jesus, the Son of God, died for his sin.* John 3:16 explains this well. Explain that God sent Jesus to die for our sin. Briefly review the Easter story. Because Jesus died, your son's sins can be forgiven. Your son must believe this is true. When he believes this, he is saved from hell and will go to heaven. Acts 16:31 and Romans 5:8 are two other good verses to read.

● *He must confess that Jesus is Lord.* Explain to your son that a Christian is someone who follows and obeys Jesus. Read Romans 10:9. A Christian asks Jesus to take charge of his life. Jesus becomes his friend. Prayer is talking to Jesus. Jesus talks to us through the Bible.

When you have explained these things, be sure your son understands. Then ask him if he really wants to take this step.

160

This is not an expression of doubt; you just want him to make his own decision.

If he says yes, then pray with him. If he can pray in his own words, encourage him to do so. Otherwise, have him repeat a prayer that you recite. Include the three "musts" discussed in this section in the prayer. Conclude with your own prayer.

Have your son describe his conversion to someone else—perhaps his mother. That will help reinforce his decision.

How can I build love and respect for the Bible in my son? Your personal example is the best way. Seeing you reading the Bible regularly and studying it for guidance in family decisions makes an impact. Your participation in a Bible study group or in teaching a Sunday school class signifies your interest. Even your physical handling of your own Bible and where and when you carry it are important influences on your son's attitude toward the Bible.

Giving your son his own Bible is another good way to build respect for the Word. By the second or third grade, your son can start reading the Bible with understanding. He should have a good Bible and be taught how to use and take care of it. Prior to this age, a small, inexpensive New Testament is adequate to make your son feel that he has one, too. As your son gets older, Bible study helps (e.g., concordance, dictionary, commentaries) are good gifts.

A third method is creative family activities with the Bible. Bible quizzes, games, songs, puppets, memory verse contests, plays, craft projects, map studies, and illustrations are all ways to have fun together. Many of these resources can be obtained in local Christian bookstores.

Fourth, read the Bible regularly to your boy. After the evening meal is a good time. With preschoolers, reading Bible stories or just talking to a toddler about a Bible picture is sufficient. In this way, you make the Bible central in your home. Some suggestions on Bible storybooks are found on page 193.

How can I help my children pray? Your son can pray as

soon as he can talk. If he understands that prayer is just talking to Jesus, he can talk to Him just as he talks to you. Children learn more about praying by doing it with you than through any kind of formal instruction. Cultivate this kind of "talking with Jesus." Sentence-long prayers are particularly good.

There are several kinds of prayer to which your child should be exposed. Prayers of confession humble the heart and clear the conscience before God. Thanksgiving prayers express gratitude and praise. Intercessory prayers express concern for others. Personal request prayers can be made for simple, everyday needs.

An average day provides many opportunities for prayer, especially for young children: before meals, before going to bed, after punishment, after a serious talk, and during family devotions. For preschoolers, short, spontaneous prayers are best. Simply suggest a prayer when you think it is suitable. Older children can appreciate more formal times of prayer, although they should know about praying silently and frequently (1 Thessalonians 5:17-18). A family prayer log can help your child see specific answers to prayer; it is important for him to learn that God does answer specific prayers.

There are many other occasions for praying with your children: in the car before a trip, on the way to church, when a family relative or friend is in need, after visits with friends, and on special holidays such as Christmas or Easter.

Make prayer a routine part of your family life.

Should I force my teenage son to attend church? This is a tough question. You can justifiably argue that as long as he lives in your house, he must attend (the same applies to other church activities). The best criterion for making a decision is to ask yourself: Will I fulfill my spiritual leadership responsibility by making him attend or by allowing him not to? You could go either way, depending on the needs of your son.

Some fathers allow their sons to attend evangelical churches other than their own if they meet their sons' needs (e.g., for larger youth groups). Other fathers determine an age at which their sons may choose, usually around fifteen or sixteen. Obviously, it is better if your son chooses on his own to attend church rather than because of your coercion. You may have to allow him some freedom to make this choice.

Are daily family devotions a requirement? No. Probably those families that have devotions together every day are in a distinct minority. And not all of those who do have daily family devotions enjoy that time together. But failing to do anything is a bad alternative.

Most families have opted for a formal devotional time once or twice a week, usually after the evening meal. Also popular is the once-a-week family night in which the devotional is combined with a family activity. Some distinction needs to be made between a devotional time, which involves discussion and teaching, and simply reading the Bible and praying. The latter is easier to do on a daily basis.

The best solution seems to be to fit formal times in as the schedule permits and take advantage of more informal, natural teaching opportunities.

What are the best methods for family devotions? There are several things that make this time enjoyable.

• The opportunity to talk freely is important. If your family does not talk freely at any other time, it will not talk freely during devotions. But having questions to discuss and permitting your child to say what is on his mind can make this time valuable.

• For younger children (under twelve), activities that are physical or that challenge mental alertness are good. Doing something is always more fun than just talking. Even a simple living-room game can help.

• Try a variety of approaches. Keep your children guessing. A list of ideas is provided in the resource section.

• If you sense that your boy is getting restless, draw the time to a close. Avoid lectures on topics of interest to you. If you end the time when everybody is still enjoying it, they will be back for more.

How do I handle the age differences of my children? Should I force my children to take part? Most of the ideas you will find for family devotions (pages 191-93) work best for children of elementary-school age. Those children can read the Bible and enjoy creative Bible activities. Most of the devotional ideas are suitable for this age level.

Preschoolers have difficulty paying attention for long periods of time. If there are older children, the preschoolers cannot handle the level of discussion. Sometimes it is better to let the younger ones simply be casual participants. Let them take part in what they like; otherwise, let them play or look at a book. Individual bedtime devotions are usually more effective for preschoolers. Because your wife is with the child most of the day, you should lead the bedtime devotions.

Teenagers need to be treated with similar flexibility. Occasionally let them take charge of the devotional time, if possible. Teaching younger children is good leadership experience. Because of school and church activities, you may have to permit teenagers to skip devotions on certain evenings. Work this out with them. You can replace those family devotions for them with personal chats with each one, perhaps based on some personal Bible study they are doing. If all your children are teens, arrange a suitable time for a more in-depth Bible study or discussion with them of a relevant Christian book.

SEVENTEEN

How to Guide Your Son Toward a Career

You are the door to your son's introduction to the world of adult living and work. Your work habits and occupation contribute to his early impressions of what adults do and what he will do when he grows up. How you relate to people from different occupations who come to your house or whom you meet with your son helps determine your son's attitude toward those careers. You are also a key person in your son's planning when he is old enough to make career decisions. This chapter describes how you can be a helpful person.

Before your son reaches adolescence, your primary task is to acquaint him with work as an occupation and daily experience. Begin by letting him visit you at your job. If possible, have him spend some time with you watching you work (four years of age is a good time since he is not yet in school). Talk to him about your job, how you earn money for the family, and what you enjoy about your job. Be careful about what you say about your work when you come home in the evening. You are portraying an attitude toward work that your son is absorbing.

You can also expose your son to a wide variety of occupations. Make a point of visiting different work locations: a fire station, city hall, an auto repair garage, a police station, and factories. Just taking him along on routine chores will also expose him to a variety of jobs.

Adolescence is the critical period in your son's life in which you can play an important role. Your son will be thinking seri-

"Son, did you say you repaired the radiator hose with—
bubblegum?"

ously about various vocations, although with some uncertainty. It is important for him to look at different possibilities. You can help by exploring the alternatives with him. Avoid trying to steer him into the career of your preference. Ask him questions to get him thinking about the implications of his choice.

You can give your son more in-depth exposure to various occupations by arranging visits for him with friends of yours in those occupations. An afternoon in a dentist's office, in a courtroom with a lawyer, or on a building site with a construction foreman can be invaluable.

As your son obtains information from various sources (e.g., the Air Force, a Bible college, or a voluntary service) and gets input from his high school guidance counselor, you can help him organize his ideas and begin evaluating the alternatives. Although the final decision is his, you can assist by clarifying for him the choices he has.

Talking to your boy about God's will at this stage is very meaningful. In prayer, you and your son can ask God for wisdom and guidance in making the right decision (James 1:5). There are many avenues in which a young man can serve the Lord. What is most important is that he live according to the will of God, as revealed in the Scriptures, in whichever direction he goes.

Choosing a College

As your son prepares to graduate from high school, he will probably feel pressured to continue his formal education because many of his friends plan to continue their formal education. In fact, more than half of all high school graduates go on in formal schooling.

Your son can choose between several kinds of schools: a Christian liberal arts college, a Bible college or school, or a secular university or college.

Certain criteria for making a decision will be important for your son. You can help him answer these questions:

167

• What will be best for my Christian growth at this time? Am I ready to take my stand as a Christian in a non-Christian setting? Or will I grow more in a Christian school, with supportive Christian teachers and students? (A change is usually good after high school. A boy from public school probably needs the Christian college, whereas a boy from a parochial school probably needs a secular university.)

• Which kind of school can help me most with my future career plans?

• Which school can I afford? Will I be strapped with school debts for many years?

• What are my friends doing? Do I prefer a friendly community of Christians, or am I ready for the large, mostly non-Christian university?

A further way to help your son decide on a school is to take him on personal visits to the schools he is considering. Normally, this should be done in the beginning of his final year in high school. Most schools welcome visiting high school students. Look over the campuses and attend some classes. Seeing the schools in person can often clinch a decision.

ALTERNATIVES TO COLLEGE

The knowledge and awareness needed for a successful career can be obtained in many ways other than spending four years in a college. Colleges provide academic learning, most of which is forgotten. But the things that most college graduates remember about college—their friends, life in a dormitory, and campus activities—can be experienced just as well in a volunteer service assignment, at a job, or by traveling with friends.

Few people are self-motivated enough to study on their own to gain the kind of academic learning a college provides. For those young people who have a "love for learning" (and can afford it), college is probably good. Whether it is good for all those who choose to attend college is another question. That only 50 percent of those entering college graduate indicates

168

that many who choose to attend college make the wrong choice.

If a college education has its weaknesses, what are the alternatives? What else can a young man do to be successful in life?

Several good options are available. A young man deserves to be fully and fairly informed of those options. A first alternative to college is occupational training. There are some ten thousand private occupational schools in the country providing specialized training in all areas of agriculture, visual arts, construction, electronics, health care, printing, transportation services, and a host of other career fields. About five million students attend the two-year schools, either full-time or part-time. Nearly one thousand two-year community colleges also provide a wide variety of occupational programs for two million students.

The goal of the occupational schools and community colleges is the same: give a young person the practical training he needs to get started in a career. Close to 80 percent of occupational-school graduates are placed in the occupations for which they were trained.

Besides successful placement of graduates, these schools have other advantages. They are cheaper than college. A year's tuition and fees range from $300 to $1650. Their programs take only two years to complete. (Those two years at a community college can be applied as credit toward a four-year college degree.) Study is concentrated on the occupational skill, and courses are taught by experienced instructors. A graduate of these schools will be skilled in his occupation and can expect to receive respect and compensation for his skill.

Perhaps the biggest advantage of occupational schools is that many of the occupations that look promising for the future require occupational training. Job openings in law, medicine, engineering, and teaching do not look promising for the next decade. But jobs for paraprofessionals—people who can perform some of the routine tasks of the professionals—should be plentiful. Some of these jobs are physician's assistant, computer technician, computer programmer, fashion designer, legal assistant, and medical-support worker. A college degree is not needed for these jobs, but specialized training is required.

A second alternative to college is an apprenticeship in a trade. There are about three hundred fifty occupations in the country in which one can be apprenticed. Those jobs are mostly in the construction and manufacturing industries, and in other work involving manual labor. An apprentice works on the job and learns the trade at night. When he completes his program and receives his journeyman's card, his salary usually jumps substantially.

Not only are salaries good in the trades, but the potential for advancement is excellent. About 35 percent of apprenticeship graduates reach management positions. Opportunities for leadership in the trade unions are always abundant, too.

Volunteer service is a third option that has become popular among many Christian young men. A common complaint about college life is that students feel useless and unproductive. Volunteer service is a good antidote for that feeling. In fact, some colleges are now incorporating volunteer service into their degree programs. Volunteer service gives a Christian young man a chance to live out his Christian commitment.

There are more options. Military service has its advantages and disadvantages. Working to save money for some future vocational effort is another excellent choice. Traveling for a year is a luxury, but well worth the money if a young man can afford it.

Make sure your son knows all the options. Encourage him to investigate them fully, and stand with him in his final decision.

For some helpful resources in career planning, see the resource section.

170

EIGHTEEN

How to Help Your Son in School

School is a major influence in your son's life. It occupies a central place in his growth years and utilizes the most productive hours of his day and year. It is a force with which you must reckon.

Whether your son attends a public or a parochial school, you should know what he is learning and doing. That information will help you decide if he is receiving the best possible education. It will also be an area in which you should relate to your son as a friend and helper.

School is an important influence on your son, and you deeply influence how well he succeeds in school. There is a direct connection between his academic progress and your involvement with him. In almost every case, a boy who does well in school has a positive attitude about his father because of his father's involvement with him. Boys who do not perform well invariably have uninvolved fathers who do not place much value on education.

There are two elements in your influence on your son's school performance: (1) your attitudes about education and personal achievements; and (2) your involvement with your son when he is in school. Exploring both these elements will yield a profitable list of actions that you can take.

WHAT YOUR ATTITUDE CAN DO

Your positive attitude about learning can make your home

"Dad, I thought everybody knew EMC^2 $\times \dfrac{23}{4 \times 5} = 0$."

a place in which learning is enjoyable. In this kind of atmosphere, discovering new information and ideas is encouraged. When your son tells you about something he found (e.g., a bird's nest), you respond enthusiastically. Letting your family know about your new discoveries also helps.

Remember that you are the expert on your child, not the school or the teacher. You know your son much better than they. If you do not like what is going on, talk to the teacher or principal. The school exists for the child, not the child for the school. Maintain the attitude of expecting the school to deliver.

Determine your expectations for your son's academic performance, and tell him what they are. Do you want your son to get good grades? stay out of trouble? learn something that will help him in a future career? enjoy learning for the sake of personal growth? What you expect is what you get.

Encourage your son to be creative. You can start doing this when he is a baby. Let him try things on his own and persevere at them. As he gets older, urge him to do his very best. Congratulate him when he develops his own idea. Originality should always get high marks. Give verbal recognition for work well done. All this builds independence and satisfaction in his own work.

Develop a healthy attitude toward reading. Many teachers claim that if a child does not read well by the second grade, he probably never will. You can help make sure your son can read well by having plenty of children's books in your house. Give books as gifts from the first birthday on. Read to him frequently. You and your wife should read to him once a day on an average. Make sure you read yourself—it is a good example for your son and better for you than watching television. Go to the library as a family when your boy is old enough.

How to Get Involved

Your son's homework presents a great opportunity for you to get involved with him. You can help him develop good study

173

habits, especially in grade school and junior high). Make sure he has a good place to study, with proper lighting and reasonable quietness. A little home-maintenance work may be necessary. Help him arrange a study schedule, and then force him to stick to it. Show interest in the homework itself. Find out what his actual assignments are each night, and check to see that he has completed them. If he has difficulty, talk to him about the assignment. Make suggestions, but do not do the work for him.

In high school and college, your son will make many decisions about courses and majors. You can give him feedback on his thoughts as he considers those decisions. Help him evaluate the pros and cons of various courses. Encourage him to decide in terms of his long-range goals.

Talk about school around the dinner table. Ask your son, "What was the highlight of your day?" or "What was the most exciting thing that happened to you today?" If problems emerge with schoolwork or schoolmates, pray about them together.

Recognize that going to school is only one way in which your son is receiving an education. The educational experiences you provide for your family are just as important. Family educational experiences can include such things as family trips to different places in the country; visits to other countries; tours of museums, historical sites, and tourist attractions; and attendance at festivals, fairs, and community events. Seeing how other people live, work, and worship helps broaden your son's education. Plan to visit some of these places, events, and attractions.

Get to know your son's teacher. Attend at least one parent-teacher conference during the school year. Express your support to her (or him), and ask her for insights about your son. Treat her as a source of information. Involvement in the local PTA or even the school board is also important. More men are needed in those organizations to balance the strong female presence. In the lower grades, women teachers outnumber men heavily, by as much as fifty to one. The time has come for an

174

aggressive role for fathers in the educational decision-making process.

Regulate your son's television viewing habits. Television tends to create a passive attitude in viewers. The mind is not active. Counteract this effect by limiting the amount of time your boy spends watching television. For the grade-school boy, a maximum of two hours per school day and ten hours on weekends is suggested. Talk about what he is viewing. Always make sure you know what he is watching.

"OK, dad, now let me stand on your head."

NINETEEN

How to Relate to Your Daughter

You may be getting the impression that the father-son relationship is special. It needs to be emphasized, and it is a good place for fathers to start learning, but it should be viewed in the context of the total family unit. The mother-son relationship is just as important. And so is the father-daughter relationship.

Much of what is said in this book applies to being a father to girls as easily as it does to being a father to boys. But there are some unique features to the father's relationship with the girl, a relationship that is extremely important.

WHY YOU ARE IMPORTANT

A brief overview of how you influence your daughter will show why you are important to her.

You influence your daughter's ability to relate to other men. Since you are the first man in her life, she gets an impression of what men are like from you. Your acceptance of her helps her feel positive about being female and tells her that men are worthwhile persons.

Your relationship with her determines the quality of her marriage to a large extent. A close, warm, father-daughter relationship will usually result in a stable marriage for the girl. Because she trusts and loves you, she will find it easy to be romantic and trusting toward the man she marries.

Girls who do not have affectionate, loving fathers often have great difficulty in their marriages. Divorce rates are higher for women who have been deprived of a loving father than for those who have not been similarly deprived.

Father absence (and severe neglect) can lead to results even more severe than divorce for many women. According to one survey, the vast majority of prostitutes come from fatherless homes. In British studies, most women convicted of major crimes report the same background. And numerous studies indicate that female homosexuality arises from this same lack of fatherly love. Those women—prostitutes, convicts, and homosexuals—were unable to receive the male affection they needed for normal growth.

You are an important balance to the influence of your wife. A dominant mother and a weak, uninvolved father can result in a daughter's disdaining and distrusting men. This attitude will usually lead to problems in her future marriage. Your having a good relationship with your wife helps your daughter develop her personality normally. She can learn comfortably from both of you. If there is tension, she is confused about the husband-wife relationship.

You affect your daughter's career choice. A warm relationship with her and your wife will help her look forward to the role of a wife and mother. Poor relationships may result in her not wanting to be tied to a home.

WHAT YOU CAN DO

Be warm and affectionate toward your daughter. Do not worry about sexual overtones. A hug and kiss or sitting close on the couch are appropriate. Let her know that you love her. Give her compliments and praise her accomplishments. Girls without this kind of affection, especially in their early years, often become "boy crazy" when they reach the teen years. Their search for male attention leads to silly behavior.

Prepare your daughter to be independent. Make sure she learns tasks that will help her in adulthood, whether she marries or not. Do not protect her from tasks that you think are only for boys. How to change the oil in a car and a flat tire are important for girls to know, too.

Talk to her about men. When she is reaching puberty, explain how boys think and act. Warn her of dangers, and give her suggestions for relating to boys. Tell her about men's needs and responsibilities, especially in marriage.

Let your daughter see the close relationship you have with your wife. Treat your wife with respect and admiration. Take your God-given family leadership role while encouraging your wife to develop her own goals and interests. Seeing these things will help your daughter to understand the proper husband-wife relationship and look forward to marriage.

TWENTY

What Happens When You Are the Only Parent

No book on being a father can overlook the plight of a special kind of father—the single father. It is hard enough to be a father when you know your wife is doing the big part of raising your child. It is another matter when you have no wife at all.

If you are a single father, you have company. Estimates by some researchers indicate that more than half a million families in the United States have the father as the only parent. This compares to almost five million families in which the mother is the only parent.

In the majority of cases, the single fathers are widowers. But there are other reasons, too, for the increasing number of fathers who are trying to hold a family together by themselves. In recent years, more wives than husbands have deserted their families. And although most divorce settlements still give the children to the mother, fathers are now winning custody of their children more than they did in the past.

There are likely few instances of Christian fathers whose wives deserted or divorced them. The Christian father usually faces the task of rebuilding his family upon the grief of his wife's death.

THE SINGLE FATHER'S PECULIAR PROBLEMS

CHILD CARE

The most obvious problem for the single father is the care of his children. Your choices for supervision may be limited. A relative often takes the responsibility. You may not be ready to handle the new fatherly tasks that have been thrust upon you, having relied heavily upon your wife. What child care you do provide is usually minimal. You may not have the time or energy to do the things that help your children grow and mature. Nor is the adjustment easy for the children, especially if they are young.

LONELINESS

The loss of a spouse through death always takes its toll and leaves the bereaved feeling very much alone. The impact of the death of a loved one never really leaves a person, either. Friendships with other couples may not be easy to maintain without your partner; the loss of your wife eliminates your identity as a couple. Being single again, you may not desire to associate with married couples (assuming you can afford the time).

REJECTION

For fathers who lost their wives through desertion or divorce, there is the stigma of a marriage that failed. If you are such a father, your own guilt feelings or even bitterness will add to this stigma, or sense of rejection. You will find yourself treated as the father of a "broken family." Developing family unity is very hard when everybody assumes that the family is destroyed.

LACK OF PERSONAL FULFILLMENT

The father who carries the burden of providing for and raising his children alone cannot devote much time to outside activities. Your social contacts will be limited. Further education and special interests must be put off. Feelings of depression may arise as you see only hard work and sacrifice ahead.

LACK OF SUPPORT

Single parents are still a neglected group within our society, and evangelical churches are even more guilty of this neglect

181

than society as a whole. Some social groups have formed for single parents (e.g., Parents Without Partners), although they are dominated by the divorced and separated. Churches have started to respond to the needs of unmarried adults. Little has been said about single parents, however, who have difficulty associating with both unmarried and married adults.

WHAT YOU CAN DO

There are positive steps a single father can take. One is to remarry. Unlike most single mothers, most single fathers are able to remarry and start to regain what they lost. Some men may not do this immediately. They can improve their lives in several ways.

Begin by preparing yourself to be a more effective father. You must do the job of two parents. It is a challenge worth tackling. The skills of being a parent can be learned. Reading a book like this is one way to prepare. Family-education experiences, counseling, and just talking to friends are other ways.

Work at a personal relationship with each child. A top priority should be friendships with your children. Your friendship will sustain them through the grief of their mother's death. It will also keep the family together during hardships and loneliness.

Establish meaningful social relationships outside the home. Squeeze a fellowship group of some kind into your schedule. You need this outlet to maintain a balanced life. You especially need to become involved in a local church. A church contains many resources you need (e.g., babysitting, health care, teaching, and financial help), although they will not be volunteered if the church does not know of your need.

Learn to handle feelings of loneliness, guilt, and bitterness. The loss of your wife through death, divorce, or desertion must be accepted. You must come to terms with it and move on alone. Pastoral counseling or talking with a close friend can help you cope with those feelings.

TWENTY-ONE

What Happens When Your Relationship with Your Son Breaks Down

If there is a fear that every father knows, it is the fear of having his son turn against him. To see a boy reject the values and standards he has been taught, including the Christian faith, can devastate a father and overwhelm him with despair and guilt.

Most young fathers probably pray that this will never happen to them. Yet as older fathers can testify, it happens frequently. You can reach the point at which you really believe you have wrecked the whole thing and then you stamp yourself as a failure.

There are at least two ways in which your relationship with your son can break down. One is primarily your doing; the other is your son's. There are steps you can take to cope with both of those failures.

WASTED YEARS

You and your son may seem miles apart emotionally simply because you did not spend time with him when he was younger. Now that he is a teenager, he does not have time for you. As you look back, you can see all kinds of opportunities that you had to do things with your son. But now it is too late, or at least it seems that way.

183

You must be careful in your evaluation of your past performance. It is always possible to think that you could have done more. No father will be totally satisfied with his efforts. But if your job and other interests took priority over your son, and he is clearly resentful toward you because of that, then you probably have created the problem.

The first step to take in rebuildling your relationship with your son is that of the publican in Luke 18:9-14. Tell God that you have failed and that you want His forgiveness and direction.

The next step is a little harder. Sit down with your son privately, tell him that you failed him by ignoring him in favor of other things, and ask him to forgive you. Tell him that more than anything else in the world, you would like to have a close relationship with him again. Ask him for his ideas on what to do. He will probably be so surprised that he will not know what to say. (One of the most common complaints teens have about their fathers is that they never apologize.) Or he will say, "Oh, that's all right." But you cannot leave it at that. You need his forgiveness (You must ask, "Will you forgive me?"), and you need his help.

The third step is to start getting to know your son again. The key to doing that is your son's interests. Whether he likes basketball, backpacking, or basket weaving, you can probably help him in some way. He may need some equipment, transportation, or just someone to cheer him on.

Getting involved in your son's interests will cost you chunks of time and force you to rearrange your schedule. Perhaps it will take a while for you to make such an involvement part of your routine, but if your son knows you are working on it, he will act differently.

As you begin to nourish a new relationship, bear in mind that your fatherly tendency to refuse to apologize and to get mad will call for frequent repentance—to God and to your son. You can crush a budding relationship with one prideful storm of

184

anger. But you can also recover the lost ground by quickly repenting.

Here are three sources of help to tap as you learn to get into touch with your son. The first is your wife; she will probably be a gold mine of information. Your son probably turned to her when you turned away from him years ago, so she has been trying to do your job and hers, too.

The second source of help is your pastor, or other men in the church. You are not the first father to face this problem; others have walked the path before you, and God has guided them to higher ground. So check with others likely to know who has done what already.

Third, read some books. The resource section in the back of this book (pages 195-96) has many suggestions.

There is a sense in which it is never too late to build a relationship with your son. When he is an adult, the relationship will be on different terms than before. But it is possible even then to build a relationship.

He Is His Own Man

A more difficult experience for fathers to handle than having failed as fathers is being rejected by their sons even when they have tried to do a good job.

If this has happened to you, you must understand that your fatherly role is a stewardship that has been entrusted to you. God has given you about eighteen years to influence your son toward mature Christian adulthood. What you can do for him will be done then. After that, he is on his own. If you have done your best to fulfill your responsibilities as a father, you have been a good steward.

All this may not be very encouraging if your son decides he does not want to live according to the values you have taught him. You have been a faithful, involved father—just what this book calls for—and yet your son rejects you. No wonder you ask yourself, "Where did I go wrong? How could this happen?"

It is not easy to explain this phenomenon, and it does not help when you hear the criticism of other parents who are convinced you must have done something wrong. One thing is certain. When your son reaches the end of high school, he has to make his own decisions. He is then responsible for his own life. He is free to choose any way of life. There is not much you can do to stop him from choosing a particular way.

That he has chosen differently from what you had wished (e.g., common-law marriage) is not necessarily a reflection on your fatherhood. It is an indication of the freedom God has given him.

God is faithful to His people, however, and you can hang on to His promise to be faithful to you and your child. Your son's rebellion may be transitory. If he accepted Christ at one point in his life, you can count on God's faithfulness to him.

Ultimately, you, like every Christian father, must depend on God. If you are an involved father who teaches his child God's values, in all likelihood your child will follow in God's way. But that is no ironclad guarantee. When your child reaches adulthood, he must make decisions for himself. You, the father, can only pray and trust in the faithfulness of your heavenly Father.

PART 4

SPECIAL INTERVIEWS

TWENTY-TWO

Joe Bayly

Joe Bayly is the vice-president of David C. Cook Publishing Company in Elgin, Illinois. He and his wife, Marylou, have four children: Debra, Tim, David, and Nathan. All four have graduated from high school and are pursuing careers. Joe has also lost three sons through death, and he describes that ordeal in his book *The View from a Hearse* (Cook, 1969). His daughter contributed a chapter to the book *What They Did Right* (Tyndale, 1974), which describes a group of successful parents.

H & R: What effect has the loss of your three sons had on the kind of parent you are?

BAYLY: We have a much closer family. I'm inclined to be affectionate anyway, but I became much more affectionate. The deaths were a freeing experience for me. I used to look for other people's approval. Now I'm relatively unconcerned about what other people think. There is a tendency, especially if you are a Christian worker, to bear down hard on your children because you are worried that their behavior will affect people's perceptions of you. This can be harmful for your children, who need the freedom to establish their own identities.

H & R: How would you describe your role as a father?

BAYLY: It changes in your life and in the lives of your children. In the beginning, you are part of the child-raising team. The mother has more opportunity to put in the Christian training in the early ages, but in later years, it's necessary for fathers to make their input.

Now that my kids are independent, it's a tremendous joy to meet them on an adult level and have fellowship with them. You never get over your responsibility for your children. They need you in various ways no matter how old they are.

I like a quotation from Schweitzer, who in later years said, "My father is my dearest friend." That is the best thing my kids could say about me when they get independent.

H & R: What approach have you used for your children's spiritual growth?

BAYLY: We have daily Bible reading and prayer after the evening meal. We read a chapter from the Bible, alternating between the Old and New Testaments. Then everyone prays. I've never been especially creative about this. We started when our children were young. They have accepted this as what our family does and have not rebelled against it.

At times of crisis and loss, we found that it was the daily Bible reading and prayer that held the family together. The children realized we weren't adrift.

Let me say that I would put other family activities on a par with this. A family devotional time doesn't run the family; rather, it's one means of glorifying God in the family.

H & R: How do you view masculinity?

BAYLY: Masculinity and femininity are not watertight categories. They are symbolically different. There are a lot of overlapping, human characteristics. But a woman's nine months of pregnancy imply a dependence on someone else's caring. I think the husband's role is to care for her. But there are also times when the husband is dependent on the wife.

There are men's and women's roles in marriage. In the family, God has designed the man to be in leadership — just like a corporation needs a president. But the chief executive is foolish if he doesn't listen to those down the line.

190

I don't find dominance in the Bible. The basic teaching is unity in marriage. The husband and wife are one flesh.

H & R: How can a busy father arrange his schedule to make time for his children?

BAYLY: Schedule things so you are not gone for long periods of time, or on weekends when the children are home. I have taken my children along on my trips. Watch your time in the home. Watching television and reading the newspaper can take time from the children.

You have to determine priorities in your church involvement. A good pastor will be interested in his fathers and mothers in the congregation, and may ask them to drop out of certain jobs to be at home more.

Sometimes a man has to turn down a promotion or avoid certain assignments. Some men may even change occupations for the sake of their families. I think this is a Christian response.

H & R: What do you say to a father who believes he has failed?

BAYLY: All of us have failed at times. I can't say I've always been the father I should've been. God in His grace has met some of the lacks I have.

When one of my sons had a rough time several years ago, my wife had to remind me constantly to have faith in God. The just shall raise their children by faith.

TWENTY-THREE

Gil Beers

Gil Beers is the author of forty children's books, including the popular Muffin Family series (Moody Press), the Learning to Read from the Bible series (Zondervan), and the ten-volume *Family Bible Library* (Southwestern). Gil and his wife, Arlie, have five children and live in Elgin, Illinois.

H & R: Gil, what specific things do you do as a father to encourage the spiritual growth of your own children?

BEERS: We have found one of the richest sources for spiritual growth to be the impromptu or spontaneous moments. We try, as most parents do, to have some regular kind of Bible reading, quizzing, and fun time together. However, we find this to be difficult to maintain consistently simply because of the diversity in the ages of our children and the intricate scheduling that is necessary with the children involved in one activity or another. To find a time is almost impossible for us, so we depend a good deal on those spontaneous moments.

I can think of one time in particular when we took a family weekend retreat at one of the state parks. We sat down together on a log out in the woods, and as we looked around and saw God's handiwork, we discussed what the various things in nature meant to us in terms of God's hand upon our lives. It was very beautiful to see how each of the children could pick out something in the woods and compare it to God's work within him or her.

Often the times you might call "down time" can be very useful for spiritual interaction. These are times when family members are forced to be together, like cleaning in the kitchen, riding in the car, Dad doing some chores with son helping, and so on. Families don't often redeem these times together.

H & R: Have you ever tried to "force" devotional times?

BEERS: Yes, we do this sometimes. The problem with the forced situation, however, is that it often is not the richest time together. Sometimes it does work out to be very valuable, but the mind is usually locked in gear to be elsewhere. Of course, the ideal is to get up at 6:00 A.M. and have a devotional time together before breakfast. Unfortunately, ideals do not always prevail.

H & R: What would you say to a father who either doesn't think he needs to lead family devotional times, or simply because he is such a busy person he has difficulty finding the time?

BEERS: I would encourage the man to read the newspaper and get a feeling for the trend in America's young people and young adult life today. If a father thinks he doesn't have the time to interact with his children, I guess I would ask him, What does he want his children to be when he's finished with them? He has x number of years with his children, and that's all. As a matter of fact, many people think we have eighteen years with our children, but we don't. By the time the child is in junior high, the die is cast, so to speak. From that point on, you're guiding in a very different way. We have found that by the time the children have left elementary school, you have done the most that you can do. Not that you don't have any influence on them in the junior high and high school years, but there are many other potent forces that come into play that will compete with your influence.

Sometimes it's not the number of hours we spend with our children that matters, but the intensity with which we are with them when we do have the time. My son Ron and I were talking about this the other evening. He said, "You know, Dad, when you're with me, *you're with me*. I feel that you are not rushing ahead to be somewhere else. You're there, and when we're talking, I feel like you're with me 100 percent."

There are people I know, and you've experienced people like this; you can start to talk with one of them, and after a moment you feel as though he's rushing somewhere else in his mind. He's not really with you in mind and spirit.

Children having this experience with a father or a mother will probably throw up their hands and say, "Well, they're not interested in me, anyway."

H & R: This matter of priority of time seems to be a very important part of a dad's struggle to be an effective father. So often a father doesn't think he has the time to spend with his children that he knows he should. He will often feel guilty as a result. Are there any further suggestions that you give to dads who find themselves in this struggle?

BEERS: I guess I feel very strongly on this matter of intensity that Ron mentioned. There are, admittedly, dads who have jobs that take them away from home, and they don't have many hours that they can spend with their children. But I think that when one of those fathers comes home and the child feels as though his father is too wrapped up in his own interests and concerns, then it's sort of a hopeless feeling for the child. My urging for a father is—when he does set aside whatever time he can, even if it's only ten or fifteen minutes, or only time for a passing comment from the child—he needs to make a conscious effort to direct his attention to his son. Make your son feel as though you're really interested in him.

We all get busy, and our minds are often dwelling on one concern or another. When a child comes to us, it is often an interruption. But it's better to look at those moments as noninterruptive. In those moments, what is the greatest priority in life? Is it the thing you are doing or thinking about—which could wait? Or is it the momentary need of that child to have you involved?

Involvement is important. Interest alone is not enough. Of course parents are interested in their children, but it's the personal involvement with them that's crucial to the children.

H & R: What about the dad who finds it difficult to express his emotions, and even at times to be tender?

BEERS: Very often, a dad who is unable to express himself emotionally or tenderly comes from a nonemotional relationship in his home when he was a child. Unfortunately, our society teaches that if you're going to be a man you don't cry, nor do you show emotions or tenderness. This is out of keeping with the image of Jesus, who was a man's man and did weep and did show emotion and tenderness. I personally think that it's a point of strength in a man when he can be strong enough to think that he is not threatened by showing tears, emotion, or tenderness. He has not fully arrived in manhood when he is still afraid that he has to repress these things in order to prove he is a man. He then teaches his son, and often unconsciously, that to be a man he must also repress his emotions and tender feelings. This perpetuates the myth that in order for a man to be strong and courageous he must subdue his more tender emotions.

H & R: So then you see significant involvement with your children as a key responsibility in your role as a father.

BEERS: Seeing it as a *responsibility* may not be the best way to motivate involvement. This makes it sound like a burden. I would prefer to stress it more as a tremendous opportunity to be involved with my children. It's something that you should want to do because you see what a wonderful thing it is, and not primarily because you think you *have* to be involved out of responsibility.

H & R: Gil, you've had several children who have been very achievement oriented and have done well in school. Are there some things that you did as a father that helped your children be this way?

BEERS: We have always believed in the philosophy that there is nothing you cannot do if you just put your mind to it. For example, when Doug was thirteen, he developed an interest in politics. He formed the idea of starting a political club in Elgin to campaign for one of the senators running at that time. He even hoped to get a storefront and use that for a while. Now there is a temptation for most parents to say, "Well, look at all the problems you're going to have with this!" They will immediately begin to remind the child that he is a child, and why doesn't he go play with his marbles.

But my approach was to say, "Fantastic, let's see what you can do with it." Anything I could do to support him, I would. So Doug gathered about eighteen kids around himself and carried out a campaign for the senator. He got a storefront to use a couple times a week. They hung posters and passed out literature. The senator lost, but what a good experience the campaign was for Doug. This was probably one of the formative experiences that encouraged his ongoing interest in politics.

When Doug came to me about running for the state legislature a couple of years ago, he was a young man, twenty years old. My answer was, "Why not!" Who was to say that he would not get into the legislature? And if he didn't get in, who was to say what tremendous effect it would have upon him experientially? If he didn't try, he certainly would not get in. If he did try and did not get in, he was prepared to accept the value of that experience and move on to something else.

We have always believed much in both incentives and encouragement. During our children's early years we had an incentive program for reading. Each book read earned so many points. A classic or very special book would, for example, earn ten points for the reader. A popular book might

196

earn no more than one or two points. Points were not awarded until the child answered certain questions, showing that he or she not only had read the book but had grasped it.

The points were redeemed on family trips for souvenirs or other things the children considered important, or at home for special things which would promote growth in their lives.

Encouragement has been basic in our home. Both Doug and Ron, and their sisters, were encouraged daily to practice their musical instruments, do their chores, or take part in family activities. When Ron ran for the junior class presidency at Wheaton, we encouraged and supported his decision. (He won.) We likewise encouraged Doug when he ran (and won) for the job of Student Government vice-president.

Arlie read to each child daily, and together we interacted every day with each of them. We believe this is one of the most important things a parent can do for his or her children. Along with this, we have tried never to discourage our children when they believed in the impossible and wanted to try it.

If you set before the child the concept that nothing is so vast that he cannot tackle it and try, there comes a point at which he begins to think that he can do things that may seem beyond him. We too often form an image of our children that is too small, just as we often form an image of ourselves that is too small.

TWENTY-FOUR

John Drescher

John Drescher is a Mennonite pastor in Scottdale, Pennsylvania, and the author of numerous books on marriage and parenthood. He and his wife, Betty, have five children and conduct couples' retreats together. John's most recent book is *Seven Things Children Need* (Herald, 1977).

H & R: How do you approach the role of fatherhood in your ministry?

DRESCHER: When I give a message on the father's reponsibility, I like to tell what Charlie Shedd says: "The best thing a father can do for his children is love their mother." The husband-wife relationship is the primary one. If the partnership is kept strong, the parenthood takes care of itself.

I also think that parents have been clobbered during the last ten to twenty years. They are plagued with guilt feelings and operate out of fear, not faith. I helped to create this in my early ministry. My approach now is to show the little, simple things everyone can do to be good parents. Look at the possibilities.

H & R: How do you encourage the spiritual nurture of your children?

DRESCHER: The informal moments are most important. A walk in the woods, examining stones to see if they are sharp or smooth, looking at the stars—all these lead you to the feet of God. They say that by the age of fifteen, a child has asked

fifty thousand questions. These are fifty thousand opportunities to teach. Through our answers to these questions,
we convey our Christianity. Praying in the car before a trip
was something we did in our family.

H & R: How do you find these informal moments?

DRESCHER: It's not easy. I don't pretend to catch them all. We
have to keep reminding ourselves of the common and or-
dinary. It's the little things. To some it may seen unnatural
to talk about spiritual things like this. I wonder then if they
think of the Lord as a constant companion.

TWENTY-FIVE

J. Allan Petersen

J. Allan Petersen is founder and president of Family Concern, Incorporated, which is based in Wheaton, Illinois. Under his leadership, the Continental Congress on the Family was held in St. Louis in 1975, an event that marked a new emphasis on the family among evangelicals. Petersen has also written several books, and he conducts numerous seminars and conferences on family life. He and his wife raised three sons.

H & R: How does a father influence his son's concept of God?

PETERSEN: Martin Luther always had a hard time praying the Lord's prayer. When he said, "Our heavenly Father," it reminded him of his own father, who was harsh and inflexible. A father conveys an image of God to his child; the child thinks God is like his father.

It took me a long time after I was an adult to get through my heart that God was really good. In my home, I was taught rules and regulations. When I obeyed the rules, my father considered me an important person. I thought that any comfort, luxury, or enjoyment was a sin. Life couldn't be enjoyed.

But God is good. He is not a policeman or an FBI agent. He gave us life to enjoy. The father has to be good so that his child will understand that God is good.

H & R: Your ministry required you to travel much while your sons were growing. How did you handle that?

PETERSEN: We had to compensate. My wife did the greater part of rearing the boys. She played with the children, and they enjoyed her. She was a strict disciplinarian, and I knew that when I came home, there was no unfinished business. She encouraged them with positive comments and Scripture. She built me up to them when I was gone.

When I was home, we tried to make the times significant. We did special things together, even took them out of school.

When I left, I'd give them a list of responsibilities to carry out while I was gone. I'd write them and check up on them.

H & R: How do you help a man who feels guilty over his failure as a father?

PETERSEN: You have to start where you are. You can't change the past. You can't saw sawdust. Get out from under the tyranny of this past and give it to God. Then you have to consciously learn from that mistake. Don't just say, "I blew it," but identify actual points of failure and then take specific action about them. Action will give more insight.

H & R: Many young fathers have trouble understanding their proper use of authority. What do you suggest?

PETERSEN: The father must be a leader in love. The form of the family is changeable, but the basic principles and responsibilities remain unchanged. What is important is that the father accepts his responsibility.

For example, I was gone a lot when my sons were young. I couldn't be there to lead a family altar every day. But I was responsible to see that there was one whether I was there or not.

The father's authority must be seen according to Ephesians 5: as Christ loved the church. That means serving. Everything Christ expected of the church, He first did. He wanted us to accept Him; He accepted us first. He wanted us to forgive; He forgave us first.

This authority calls for taking the initiative. It's easy to be a boss. It's tough to serve.

201

Appendix

RESOURCES FOR THE ACTIVE FATHER

How to Obtain Resources:

1. Check your local Christian bookstore. If it does not have the book, ask the clerk to order it for you.

2. Write. A postcard will do.

3. Check the public library for most of the secular books listed in this section. If the library does not have the book, the librarian can obtain it for you through a library exchange program.

FAMILY FUN

IDEAS FOR FATHERS AND SONS

Take a cross-country bike hike with your boy. Pack a lunch, start early in the morning, and head for your destination. The destination may be an interesting site or just any old spot on the map. Be sure to start back for home before it gets too dark.

Arrange ahead of time to take your son on a tour of your local police or fire station. The policemen and firemen are usually very cooperative, and your boy will enjoy it immensely.

Take a drive in the country in the autumn. See what interesting back roads you and your son can find. Stop occasionally and enjoy the fall colors. See how many colors of trees you can find. Identify as many kinds of leaves as you can. This may be a good time for you to start a leaf collection together. Pause for a moment to thank God for His beautiful creation.

Spend an hour or two and play some games with your son.

They could be your favorite family games or games your son particularly likes.

Take your son (and your other children individually as well) Christmas shopping for his mom and brothers and sisters. Treat him to a special snack stop.

Purchase a model of something for your son. Choose one that is a little more elaborate than those typical for six or seven year olds. Build it together. Perhaps this would be a good Christmas gift for your boy.

Do something of your boy's choosing with him.

Take your boy to work with you for a day. Arrange the visit ahead of time with your supervisors. You can arrange for your son to have a day off from school or wait for one of the official school days off. It is a tremendous experience for your boy to learn and see for himself what his dad does most of his daily life.

Participate with your son in some winter sport. It could be ice-skating, tobogganing, sledding, or even skiing.

Spend a couple of hours working on your car with your son. Change the oil, or change or adjust the points and plugs. Explain various parts of the car to your boy.

Make a kite with your son and fly it together.

Take your boy to some professional athletic event if you are close to a major city.

Take your son miniature golfing or to a small, nine-hole golf course. Show him how great your swing is. Your small boy probably will not be very powerful or accurate in his golfing, but the best time for him to start learning is when he is young.

Set up a tent (borrow one if you do not have one) in your backyard and sleep out with your boy. Or if you are in a warm part of the country, sleep out under the stars on a clear night. Spend some time looking at the various constellations.

Take a hike with your son into some wooded area. Take a bag lunch. Take a book that identifies edible plants, and see how many you can find. Also take a compass and be sure you do not get lost. How much wildlife can you see? To do it big, make it an overnight campout.

Go someplace special and take a swim with your boy. If he does not know how to swim, give him a few pointers to get him started.

IDEAS FOR THE WHOLE FAMILY

Beaver, Edmund. *Travel Games.* Thirty-two pages of games to play while driving on the highway. Write Beavers, LaPorte, Minn. 56461.

Chandler, Russ, and Chandler, Sandie. *Your Family: Frenzy or Fun.* Los Angeles: Acton, 1977. A collection of enjoyable family activities.

Jacobsen, Marion L. *How to Keep Your Family Together . . . and Still Have fun.* Grand Rapids, Mich.: Zondervan, 1972.

Over the River and Through the Woods. Scottdale, Pa.: *Christian Living* magazine, 1977. Activities for the traveling family. Write *Christian Living,* 616 Walnut Ave., Scottdale, Pa. 15683.

Self, Margaret, ed. *One Hundred Fifty-Eight Things to Make.* Glendale, Calif.: Regal, 1971.

————. *Two Hundred Two Things to Do.* Glendale, Calif.: Regal, 1968.

DEVOTIONAL RESOURCES

FOR FAMILY DEVOTIONS

Books

Anson, Elva. *How to Keep the Family That Prays Together from Falling Apart.* Chicago: Moody, 1975.

Bock, Lois, and Working, Miji. *Happiness Is a Family Time Together.* Old Tappan, N.J.: Revell, 1975. Gives twenty-six family interaction sessions that include Bible exploration. These sessions can set a good pattern for your family.

Dixon, Paul. *A Guide to Successful Family Devotions.* Chicago: Moody, 1977.

Johnson, Ruth I. *Devotions for the Family.* 3 vols. Chicago: Moody, 1958.

LeBar, Lois E. *Family Devotions with School-Age Children.* Old Tappan, N.J.: Revell, 1973. Gives guidelines for a profitable Bible study and discussion of personal and spiritual needs of children and teens.

Martin, Dorothy. *Creative Family Worship.* Chicago: Moody, 1976.

May, Edward. *Family Worship Idea Book.* St. Louis: Concordia, 1965. Contains planned family worship services for special occasions in the year. Different kinds of prayer and music are also included.

Richards, Larry. *Helping My Family Worship.* Cincinnati: Standard, 1977.

Rickerson, Wayne E. *Good Times for Your Family.* Glendale, Calif.: Regal, 1976. An excellent resource for Bible-related activities that teach Christian values. Rickerson presents over one hundred simple family activities in such areas as art, puzzles, word games, table activities, and Bible games that you can enjoy in your home. This book is ideal for a weekly family night.

Rinker, Rosalind. *How to Have Family Prayers.* Grand Rapids, Mich.: Zondervan, 1977. Tells parents how to teach their children to pray, and provides thirty days of family devotions that are focused on prayer.

Scanlan, Betsey, ed. *The Family Bible Study Book.* 2 vols. Old Tappan, N.J.: Revell, 1975. A collection of fifteen-minute Bible studies in various books of the Bible. Written by a dozen women, these two volumes are great for all ages.

Ward, Ruth. *Devotions: A Family Affair.* Kalamazoo, Mich.: Masters Press, 1977.

Webb, Barbara O. *Devotions for Families: Fruit of the Family.* Valley Forge, Pa.: Judson, 1974.

Periodicals

Daily Bread for Boys and Girls. Write Child Evangelism Fellowship, Inc., Box 348, Warrenton, Mo. 63303.

Family Life Today magazine. Has weekly family-night plans and daily Bible readings. Each month has a theme. See information for subscription on page 198.

Rejoice. Daily Bible-reading guide for the family with school-age children. Write Mennonite Brethren Publishing House, Box L, Hillsboro, Kans. 67063.

Miscellaneous

Creative Activity Pacs. Put out by Gospel Light, these contain Bible-related crafts for all ages and can be used on special family nights.

FOR PRESCHOOLERS

Bible storybooks

Bible storybooks are one of the best ways to begin teaching your children about God's Word. There are many to choose from. Use the following criteria for selecting which ones to buy:

- amount and style of illustrations—the more illustrations the better if they are simple and realistic
- story copy—should not be too long or hard to understand
- added help for the child—for example, questions to ask your child about the stories
- content—should be biblically accurate.

The following are excellent Bible storybooks.

Beers, V. Gilbert. *Family Bible Library*. 10 vols. Nashville, Tenn.: Southwestern, 1971. Sold only by company representatives.

Egermeier, Elsie. *Egermeier's Bible Story Book*. 5th ed. Anderson, Ind.: Warner Press, 1969.

Gross, Arthur W. *Concordia Bible Story Book*. St. Louis: Concordia, 1971.

Hook, Francis. *Jesus, The Friend of Children*. Elgin, Ill.: David C. Cook, 1976.

The Moody Bible Story Book. Chicago: Moody, 1953.

Taylor, Kenneth N. *Taylor's Bible Story Book*. Rev. ed. Wheaton, Ill.: Tyndale, 1976.

Devotional guides

Devotional guides are also written for preschoolers. They usually include a brief thought and Bible reading.

Aaseng, Rolf E. *God Is Great, God Is Good: Devotions for Families.* Minneapolis: Augsburg, 1972.

Hook, Martha, and Boren, Tinka. *Little Ones Listen to God.* Grand Rapids, Mich.: Zondervan, 1971.

Jahsmann, Allan H., and Simon, Martin P. *Little Visits with God.* St. Louis: Concordia, 1957.

LeBar, Mary. *Living in God's Family.* Wheaton, Ill.: Scripture Press, 1957.

Taylor, Kenneth N. *The Bible in Pictures for Little Eyes.* Chicago: Moody, 1956.

Children's books

Children's books can also be used as devotionals. Selecting good literature should be a careful process. Even with Christian books, some are much better than others. Gladys Hunt's *Honey for a Child's Heart* (Zondervan, 1969) is good to read with regard to choosing children's books.

Barrett, Ethel. *It Didn't Just Happen.* Glendale, Calif.: Regal, 1967. This is one of the many exciting, Bible-related stories written by the famous storyteller that you can read to your children.

Beers, V. Gilbert. *A Gaggle of Green Geese.* Chicago: Moody, 1974.

————. *Around the World with My Red Balloon.* Chicago: Moody, 1973.

————. *Cats and Bats and Things Like That.* Chicago: Moody, 1972.

————. *God Is My Helper, God Is My Friend, Jesus Is My Teacher, Jesus Is My Guide.* Learning to Read from the Bible series, vols. 1-4. Grand Rapids, Mich.: Zondervan, 1973. The four books in this series are actually reading primers.

FOR YOUR SON'S PERSONAL DEVOTIONS

Helping your son start a regular time of Bible reading and prayer is important. The best time to begin is during his junior years (ages eight to eleven).

Books

Johnson, Ruth I. *Daily Devotions for Early Teens.* 4 vols. Chicago: Moody, 1960-74.

————. *Daily Devotions for Juniors.* 4 vols. Chicago: Moody, 1964-67. An inexpensive way to get your son started.

Souter, John, and Souter, Susan. *Youth Bible Study Notebook.* Wheaton, Ill.: Tyndale, 1977. Excellent for your teenage son.

Miscellaneous

Various Bible correspondence programs for junior and junior high young people are effective. You may wish to contact the Bible Club Movement, 237 Fairfield Ave., Upper Darby, Pa. 19082.

Graded Daily Bible Reading Material, from Scripture Union, provides daily reading for children age three and older. Request a catalog. Write Scripture Union, 1716 Spruce St., Philadelphia, Pa. 19103.

Books About Fatherhood

BY MEN

Biller, Henry B., and Meredith, Dennis. *Father Power.* New York: McKay, 1975. Can be considered a classic on fatherhood. Biller has studied, researched, and written about fatherhood more than any other person. He discusses fatherhood from every angle you can think of (except a biblical angle).

Dodson, Fitzhugh. *How to Father.* New York: Signet, 1975. A mini-encyclopedia for fathers on every phase of being a parent. Full of ideas and resources, this book will keep any father busy for years.

MacDonald, Gordon. *The Effective Father.* Wheaton, Ill.: Tyndale, 1977. Probably the best book on fatherhood written by an evangelical. MacDonald, a pastor, outlines excellent principles for the Christian father to operate upon and illustrates them from his own experience.

Shedd, Charlie W. *Smart Dads I Know.* Mission, Kans.: Sheed & Ward, 1975. Takes a light, anecdotal approach. You can get some good ideas from this book.

BY WOMEN

Gilbert, Sara D. *What's a Father For?* New York: Warner Books, 1975. A little more sensational than and not as practical as Maureen Green's book.

Green, Maureen. *Fathering.* New York: McGraw-Hill, 1976. Makes a solid case for a stronger fatherly role.

FOR SCHOLARS

Benson, Leonard. *Fatherhood: a Sociological Perspective.* New York: Random, 1968.

Biller, Henry B. *Father, Child, and Sex Role: Paternal Determinats in Personality Development.* Lexington, Mass.: Lexington, 1971.

————. *Paternal Deprivation.* Lexington, Mass.: Lexington, 1974.

Lynn, David B. *The Father: His Role in Child Development.* Monterey, Calif.: Brooks-Cole, 1974.

Schaefer, George. *The Expectant Father.* Everyday Handbook Series. New York: Barnes & Noble, 1972.

PERSONAL ACCOUNTS

Several personal accounts of father-son relationships make enjoyable reading.

Bottomly, Heath. *Prodigal Father.* Glendale, Calif.: Regal, 1976.

Leenhouts, Keith J. *A Father ... A Son ... and a Three-Mile Run.* Grand Rapids, Mich.: Zondervan, 1975.

Books About Masculinity

HUMANISTIC PERSPECTIVE

There are numerous secular books that explore the impact of the feminist movement on the male identity. Most examine similar topics. Read one for your interest. You will not agree with the humanistic assumptions of these writers, but you will discover the issues that must be discussed.

Farrell, Warren. *The Liberated Man.* New York: Bantam, 1975.

Fasteau, Marc. *The Male Machine.* New York: McGraw-Hill, 1974.

Goldberg, Herb. *The Hazards of Being Male: Surviving the Myth of Masculine Privilege.* New York: Nash, 1976.

Nichols, Jack. *Men's Liberation: A New Definition of Masculinity.* New York: Penguin, 1975.

Steinmann, Anne, and Fox, David. *The Male Dilemma: How to Survive the Sexual Revolution.* New York: Jason Aronson, 1974.

CHRISTIAN PERSPECTIVE

Andrews, Gini. *Sons of Freedom.* Grand Rapids, Mich.: Zondervan, 1975. Helpful reading for the single man. Identity, self-acceptance, sexuality, and leadership are some of the topics covered in this book.

Benson, Dan. *The Total Man.* Wheaton, Ill.: Tyndale, 1977. An excellent book on Christian masculinity. Benson's approach is fresh, frank, and very practical. We highly recommend this book.

Getz, Gene A. *The Measure of a Man.* Glendale, Calif.: Regal, 1974. Getz examines each characteristic discussed in 1 Timothy 3 and Titus 1 and applies it to the Christian man's life. This book is suitable for a men's fellowship group.

Petersen, J. Allan, ed. *For Men Only.* Wheaton, Ill.: Tyndale, 1973. A collection of interesting articles.

Warner, Gary, ed. *A Special Kind of Man.* Carol Stream, Ill.: Creation House, 1973. Another collection of articles.

MAGAZINES FOR THE CHRISTIAN FAMILY

The Christian Home. Published monthly by the United Methodist Publishing House, 201 Eighth Ave., South, Nashville, Tenn. 37202. For parents of children and youth. Contains discussion guide for articles, family fun ideas, a column for single parents, and a column for married couples.

Christian Living. Published monthly by Mennonite Publishing House, 616 Walnut Ave., Scottdale, Pa. 15683. Focuses on marriage and family living. Inspirational and practical.

Dads Only. A monthly newsletter for Christian fathers. Has helpful ideas on how to be a better father. Published by Paul Lewis and Ray Bruce, P.O. Box 20594, San Diego, Calif. 92120.

Evangelizing Today's Child. Published every two months by Child Evangelism Fellowship, Inc., P.O. Box 348, Warrenton, Mo. 63383. Contains articles for children plus ideas and resources for teaching Bible truths.

Family Life Today. Published monthly by Gospel Light Publications, 110 W. Broadway, Glendale, Calif. 91204. Contains practical articles, weekly family-night ideas, and daily Bible readings.

Home Made. Published monthly by Family Concern, Inc., 1415 Hill Ave., Wheaton, Ill. 60187. A bulletin insert for Christian families. Talk to your pastor about use in your church.

Moody Monthly. Published monthly by Moody Bible Institute, 820 N. LaSalle St., Chicago, Ill. 60610. Features frequent articles for parents, a teen focus section, and a children's section.

Mushroom Family. A Christian family newsletter that contains interesting ideas and insights into alternative life-styles. Edited and published monthly by Fred Doscher, P.O. Box 12572, Pittsburgh, Pa. 15241.

Parents' Magazine. Published monthly by Parents' Institute, 80 New Bridge Rd., Bergenfield, N.J. 07621. Although the magazine is geared primarily to women, many articles are very helpful to fathers.

BOOKS ABOUT FAMILY DISCIPLINE

There is a wide range of literature on discipline written by evangelical authors. The books listed below are a sampling of that range.

Barber, Bill. *Discipline and the Young Child.* Glendale, Calif.: Regal, 1977. A small book with good insights.

Dobson, James. *Dare to Discipline.* Wheaton, Ill.: Tyndale, 1970. A popular book that recommends firm discipline. Dobson encourages the use of reinforcement methods and is a strong advocate of spanking.

Hendricks, Howard. *Heaven Help the Home!* Wheaton, Ill.: Victor, 1974. Has an excellent chapter on discipline.

Narramore, Bruce. *Help! I'm a Parent.* Grand Rapids, Mich.: Zondervan, 1972. Emphasizes personal example and the use of natural consequence. Narramore recommends spanking as a last resort.

Shedd, Charlie W. *You Can Be a Great Parent*. Waco, Tex.: Word, 1976. Represents the least conservative position. Shedd advocates a democratic approach rather than dominant fatherly leadership.

Books for Talking about Sex

Clarkson, E. Margaret. *Susie's Babies*. Grand Rapids, Mich.: Eerdmans, 1960. For young children.

Concordia Sex Education Series. St. Louis: Concordia, 1967. The best and most comprehensive Christian sex-education program available. The following four books make up the series:

I Wonder, I Wonder, by Marguerite K. Frey. For ages 5-9.
Wonderfully Made, by Ruth S. Hummell. For ages 10-12.
Take the High Road, by A. J. Bueltmann. For ages 13-16.
Life Can Be Sexual, by Elmer N. Witt. For ages 17-18.

There is also a parent's handbook for each of the four books to help you answer your children's questions.

Kehle, Mary. *You're Nearly There: Christian Sex Education for Ten-to-Teens*. Wheaton, Ill.: Shaw, 1973. For ages 10-13.

Petersen, J. Allan; Smith, Elven; and Smith, Joyce. *Before You Marry*. Omaha, Nebr.: Family Concern, 1974. A Bible-study guide for singles. Deals with sex and marriage.

Taylor, Kenneth N. *Almost Twelve*. Wheaton, Ill.: Tyndale, 1975. Good for juniors.

Vincent, M. O. *God, Sex and You*. Philadelphia: Lippincott, 1971. For teens.

College and Career Resources

BOOKS

Barron's Guide to the Two-Year Colleges. Rev. ed. 2 vols. Woodbury, N.Y.: Barron's, 1975. Look for this in your public library.

Board, Stephen et al. *HIS Guide to Life on Campus*. Downers Grove, Ill.: InterVarsity, 1973. Prepares a young, Christian man for the challenges he will face at a secular school.

College Blue Book of Occupational Education. 3d ed. New York: Macmillan, 1977. Contains descriptions of twelve thousand two-year colleges and trade and technical schools. Your public library should have a copy.

Lovejoy, Clarence E. *Lovejoy's Career and Vocational School Guide.* New York: Simon & Schuster, 1973. Look for this in your public library.

Occupational Outlook Handbook. Washington, D.C.: U.S. Bureau of Labor Statistics, 1977-78. Published every two years, but updated every three months under the title *Occupational Outlook Quarterly.* You can find a copy in your public library. The book describes eight hundred occupations and gives you this information about each: nature of the job; where you do this kind of work; what qualifications and training are needed; what the chances are of getting this job in the future; salaries and working conditions; and where you can get more information.

Webber, Robert. *How to Choose a Christian College.* Carol Stream, Ill.: Creation House, 1973. Provides guidelines for choosing a college and detailed charts for all Christian schools, showing all areas in which they offer courses.

Zehring, John William. *Get Your Career in Gear.* Wheaton, Ill.: Victor, 1976. A practical book for Christian high schoolers on choosing a career.

PERIODICALS

Moody Monthly magazine. Publishes annually (in its March issue) a catalog of Christian colleges, listing the majors offered at each school.

Venture magazine. Publishes an annual Christian college handbook. Each issue features data on over thirty Christian colleges and a response card to send in to receive packets of information about the particular colleges in which you are interested. For a free handbook, write *Venture,* P.O. Box 150, Wheaton, Ill. 60187.

ORGANIZATIONS

Intercristo. If your son is interested in Christian service, either short-term or as a career, he should contact this organization, which is an excellent referral service. Write to Intercristo, P.O. Box 9323, Seattle, Wash. 98109. There is a nominal fee for this service.

Small Business Administration. Most large cities have a regional office. There you can pick up free booklets on all aspects of small business operation, if your son is interested in going into business for himself.

U.S. Bureau of Apprenticeships and Training. There is an office in most major cities in the United States. Those offices have much information about apprenticeships that are required for many occupations, especially trades and crafts. Remember that when someone is an apprentice, he also has a full-time job.

PARENT EDUCATION OPPORTUNITIES

SEMINARS AND CONFERENCES

Creative Home Teaching Seminar. This seminar is led by Wayne Rickerson, author of *Good Times for Your Family* (see page 192). The seminar runs for six hours on a Saturday and is held in local churches. Write to Rickerson at 13600 S.W. Allen Blvd., Beaverton, Oreg. 97005.

Family Affair. This is a regional conference sponsored by Family Concern, Inc., 1415 Hill Ave., Wheaton, Ill. 60187. Well-known Christian authors on family life are featured. Details for arranging a conference in your area can be obtained from the organization.

Family Involvement Training. This is a training program for parents who want to improve their skills in building family relationships. It is sponsored by Pine Rest Life Enrichment Center, 6850 S. Division Ave., Grand Rapids, Mich. 49508, and courses are held in Grand Rapids.

GROUP STUDY MATERIALS

Building Father-Son Relationships. A seven-session course (or thirteen-week adult Sunday school elective) for fathers in a local church. A kit contains materials for ten men. Sessions can be led by the pastor or director of Christian education. Order the kit from Christian Service Brigade, P.O. Box 150, Wheaton, Ill. 60187.

The Ungame. A table game for Christian families that helps to build communication. Write to The Ungame Company, 1440 S. State College Blvd., Bldg. 20, Anaheim, Calif. 92806. Two other games produced by the same company are *Social Security Scroll* and *Roll-a-Role.*

215

The following associations can provide useful information about child development and family living. Their activities and publications are not necessarily endorsed by the authors or publisher.

Association for Childhood Education International
3615 Wisconsin Ave., N.W.
Washington, D.C. 20016

ERIC Clearinghouse on Early childhood Education
University of Illinois
805 W. Pennsylvania Ave.
Urbana, Ill. 61801
This is a national research center that can tell you everything about how children learn and develop. They have good resources on fatherhood, too.

Family Concern, Inc.
1415 Hill Ave.
Wheaton, Ill. 60187

National Council on Family Relations
1219 University Ave. S.E.
Minneapolis, Minn. 55414

Parents Without Partners, Inc.
7910 Woodmont Ave.
Washington, D.C. 20014

U.S. Department of Health, Education, and Welfare
Office of Child Development
Donohoe Bldg., 400 Sixth St. S.W.
Washington, D.C. 20201

AUDIOVISUAL RESOURCES

CASSETTE TAPES

Of special interest is a series of six tapes by James Dobson called *Preparing for Adolescence*. Dobson speaks directly to young people (ages 10-14) about inferiority, group pressure, puberty, and love. The series is an excellent discussion starter for family talks. Check

216

in your Christian bookstore or order from One Way Library (see address below).

The Navigators' *Scriptural Home Seminar* is a course for you, your wife, and other couples. It contains six cassette tapes, a leader's guide, and a workbook. Order from the Navigators (see address below).

Sources of cassette tapes on family life

● Christian Marriage Enrichment, 8000 E. Girard, Suite 602, Denver, Colo. 80231

● Creative Resources, 4800 W. Waco Dr., Waco, Tex. 76703

● Family Concern, Inc., 1415 Hill Ave., Wheaton, Ill. 60187

● Family Life, P.O. Box 1299, El Cajon, Calif. 92022

● Inspirational Tape Library, 5337 E. Earll Dr., Phoenix, Ariz., 85018

● Life Enrichment Center, 6850 S. Division Ave., Grand Rapids, Mich. 49508

● Navigators, P.O. Box 1659, Colorado Springs, Colo. 80901

● One Way Library, P.O. Box 15163, Santa Ana, Calif. 92705

Send a postcard and ask for a brochure on family-life cassette tapes.

FILMS AND FILMSTRIPS

My Son, My Son, a ninety-minute film, is a stirring, true account of a father's failure to build a relationship with his son. Rent the film from a Ken Anderson film distributor or write Ken Anderson Films (see address below).

Parents' Magazine Films has produced a good selection of filmstrips on child rearing, parenthood, and parent-teenager relations. Cassette tapes and discussion guides are also included. For more information, write Parents' Magazine Films (see address below).

Excellent Christian films are also produced by Family Films (see address below).

Sources of films and filmstrips on family life

● Family Films, 14622 Lanark St., Panorama City, Calif. 91402

● Ken Anderson Films, P.O. Box 618, Winona Lake, Ind. 46590

● Parents' Magazine Films, Dept. F, 52 Vanderbilt Ave., New York, N.Y. 10017

ORGANIZED FAMILY PROGRAMS

Christian Family Life. A church-sponsored program in which families spend one night per week together. All the materials are provided. For more information, write Family Concern, Inc., 1415 Hill Ave., Wheaton, Ill. 60187.

Sunday School Plus. A family-oriented approach to Sunday-school teaching. Developed by Larry Richards. Introductory material is available for study by a church. Write Standard Publishing, 8121 Hamilton Ave., Cincinnati, Ohio, 45231.

Tree Climbers. A father-son program for boys six and seven years old. Developed by Christian Service Brigade, P.O. Box 150, Wheaton, Ill. 60187. Features a weekly or biweekly one-hour program led by father-son teams. Each meeting includes a craft activity, games, and a ten-minute-long creative devotional. Two years' worth of materials is available.

Moody Press, a ministry of the Moody Bible Institute, is designed for education, evangelization, and edification. If we may assist you in knowing more about Christ and the Christian life, please write us without obligation: Moody Press, c/o MLM, Chicago, Illinois 60610.

HISTORY AND ROMANCE
WORKS BY HOWARD PYLE
FROM THE BROKAW FAMILY COLLECTION

Howard Pyle - A Life in Illustration
by Howard P. Brokaw

How and Why We Collected
by Howard P. Brokaw

The Exhibition
April 4 through May 17, 1998
Brandywine River Museum
Brandywine Conservancy
Chadds Ford, Pennsylvania

This publication was supported by a generous grant from The Davenport Family Foundation

Cover (detail)
(cat. 62) The Wolf and Dr. Wilkinson, 1909

Preceding page
(cat. 9) The Wreck, 1892

A Brandywine River Museum Publication
© 1998 by the Brandywine Conservancy, Inc.
Library of Congress Catalogue Number: 98-70364
ISBN 0-9663711-0-0
Second printing, 2006

Edited by Catherine E. Hutchins
Designed by Gėnė E. Harris, Karen Baumgartner,
and Diana Abreu
Photographs for the Brandywine River Museum
by Rick Echelmeyer
Electronic files by Alphabet Graphics
Printed by Pemcor, Inc Lancaster, PA

(cat. 5) **He Lay Silent and Still (He Lay Silent and Still with His Face Half Buried in the Sand)**, *1890*

Preface

"Quality is never an accident. It is always the result of intelligent effort."

— John Ruskin

As much as Howard Pyle sought quality in his art, his grandson, Howard Pyle Brokaw, seeks it in his collecting and many other endeavors. Howard Pyle established standards of excellence in illustration for his own and following generations. Howard Brokaw — collector, constant student, businessman, naturalist, conservationist, trustee of the Brandywine Conservancy and other organizations — is well known for his ready defense of standards. In times when it is not always popular to speak of standards and of quality, Howard Brokaw challenges himself and others to abide by precepts. The strength of character evident in the grandson must be like the famous fortitude of the artist as testified to by his students. In the grandson we witness a portion of Howard Pyle's character. Each man is possessed of a steadfastness of purpose.

Thirty-five years of dedication to collecting his grandfather's work has resulted in the artistic legacy Howard Brokaw offers for our pleasure. The present exhibition is a rare opportunity to see a fine collection assembled with great intelligence, the components of which demonstrate the large variety of subjects and techniques mastered more than a century ago by Howard Pyle, "the father of modern American illustration."

The Brokaw family collection, begun by Howard Pyle Brokaw and his wife, Mary (Dede) Taylor Brokaw, has expanded through the efforts of the other family members, especially son Thomas C. T. Brokaw, his wife Margaretta, and their daughters. The public has not seen the fullness of this collection before now. This is a unique exhibition the museum's trustees and staff members have long hoped to offer, and recent collecting by the Brokaws makes it a more extensive installation than it would have been previously. We are honored that it appears in our galleries and that this catalogue can represent its abundance and quality.

We are also honored by — and deeply grateful for — Mr. and Mrs. Howard Brokaw's announcement that the majority of works in their collection will be a bequest to the Brandywine River Museum. Their eventual gift gives the exhibition added distinction. The Brokaws have previously given paintings by Pyle to our permanent collection, and this enormous additional gift is thrilling and a special source of pride for all associated with this institution; it has very special meaning for George A. Weymouth, a founder of the museum, whose passion for Howard Pyle's art is well known.

The Brokaws have a passion for beautiful things, for the natural world, for history, and for their heritage rooted in old Delaware and this river valley. However, they are restrained in their pride. We offer the present publication in honor of them and with the hope that they find it at least a small reward for their wonderful dedication and generosity.

James H. Duff
Director

Acknowledgements

In the preparation of the exhibition and this publication, I have had assistance from many people to whom I am deeply grateful. My greatest thanks go to Howard and Dede Brokaw for their continuous support and encouragement and for sharing this collection. Howard Brokaw's essays regarding the art and life of Howard Pyle and the collection are wonderful contributions to the study and understanding of this region's art history.

I also thank Mr. and Mrs. Thomas C.T. Brokaw for their ready cooperation in lending many of Pyle's works and making it possible to photograph these in their home.

Appreciation is extended to staff members of the Brandywine River Museum for assistance and constructive advice, especially to James H. Duff, director; Jean Gilmore, registrar; Karen Baumgartner, assistant registrar; and Andrea Gersen, executive secretary.

My deep gratitude goes to the following members of the Brokaw Family who generously lent to this exhibition:

Mr. and Mrs. Howard Pyle Brokaw
Mr. and Mrs. Thomas C.T. Brokaw
Margaretta S. Brokaw
Phoebe Churchman Pyle Brokaw
Nicholas V.L. Brokaw
Jeffrey J. Brokaw
Clotilda Brokaw Heimbuch

All of these family members have made possible the extensive exhibition and eventual gift that will bring so much pleasure to the museum's visitors.

Gėnė E. Harris
Curator of Collections

Photograph of Howard P. Brokaw in front of a life-size photograph of his grandfather,
Howard Pyle. Photograph by Pat Crowe, Wilmington News Journal, *1973.*

Howard P. Brokaw
HOWARD PYLE—A LIFE IN ILLUSTRATION

Howard Pyle was first and foremost an illustrator — an illustrator of books and magazines. And he took great satisfaction and pride in that work. Throughout his career he retained his belief in the artistic value of book illustration and his hope for the brilliance of its future. His goal in life was to carry the torch from the great illustrators of the past — and to guide others toward carrying that torch after him.

In 1901 he told fellow members of the Bibliophile Society:

> I sometimes think that we are upon the edge of some new era in which the art of beautifying books with pictures shall suddenly be uplifted into a higher and a different plane of excellence; when ornate printed colour and perfect reproduction shall truly depict the labour of the patient draughtsman who strives so earnestly to beautify the world in which he lives, and to lend a grace to the living therein.[1]

Seven years later, in a speech to the American Institute of Architects, he said:

> For three and thirty years I have served steadfastly in my chosen profession of an illustrator. In that time I have beheld the Art of Illustration originating from the small obscure beginnings of a discredited handicraft, until today it is a dominant factor in existing

American Art. . . . the American people love to see the things that interest them made beautiful with pictured images.[2]

These words come obviously from a man inspired with a mission, and they suggest three questions: First, what fashioned Howard Pyle's inspiration and how did he build his career as a renowned illustrator and teacher of a new generation of illustrators? Second, was his concept to be realized — that concept of a brilliant future for the beautification of books through illustration? And finally, what makes his pictures effective as illustrations for books, and why are the originals of these illustrations for books being shown in an exhibit and a catalogue, far removed from the context for which they were originally created?

Howard Pyle's career began with his mother, Margaret Churchman Painter Pyle. She loved books (and wrote a few stories herself for magazines). From an early age she read to him and encouraged him to pore through the pictures in the family's library of illustrated books. *She* fashioned his inspiration — an inspiration that never left him. In an autobiographical sketch written about 1903, Pyle wrote:

> an illuminating joyfulness in beautiful things . . . brightened my early childhood . . . my mother was very fond of pictures; but especially was she fond of pictures in books. A number of pictures hung on the

*(cat.1) **The Master Caused Us to Have Some Beere**, 1883*

walls of our house . . . that were thought to be good pictures in those days. But we — my mother and I — liked the pictures in the books the best of all. I may say to you in confidence that even to this very day I still like the pictures you find in books better than wall pictures. . . .

Thus it was that my mother taught me to like books and pictures, and I cannot remember the time that I did not like them; so that time, perhaps, was the beginning of that taste that led me to do the work I am now doing. . . . I cannot remember the time when I was not trying to draw pictures.[3]

Howard Pyle was sent to private schools in Wilmington — Friends School and then Clarkson Taylor's, but he never chose to be a good student. He spent much of his time writing and sketching — with the strong encouragement of his mother. When he was sixteen and it came time to prepare for college, he demurred, and instead went to study art with a Dutch artist, trained in Antwerp, named F. A. van der Wielen, who ran a small private art school in Philadelphia.[4] For three years he studied under this apparently excellent teacher and demanding taskmaster. There he got his solid training in technique.

At the same time, Pyle educated himself through reading and observation. He steeped himself in history and fed his mind and imagination by intense study of the British and American masters of prose, poetry, and pictures. He made no serious attempt at that stage, however, to become a writer or artist. Instead he joined his father in the family leather business and, while continuing to write and draw in his spare time, he did not submit his drawings for publication.

(cat. 2) *The Wise Fools of Gotham*
(*"To Sea in a Bowl!" Exclaimed the Puzzled Pembroke*), 1886

(cat. 3) ***Coureurs De Bois in Town,*** *1888*

(cat. 4) ***The Saving of King Inge***, *1888*

(cat. 6) **On the Way to Tyburn**, *1890*

14

(cat. 52) **The Passing of Doña Victoria,** *1908*

(cat. 7) **Grandmother's Story of Bunker Hill Battle,** *1892*

16

After five years of this, at the age of 23, came the opportunity for change. In August 1876 he made a trip down the Delmarva Peninsula to Chincoteague, Virginia. He wrote "Chincoteague, the Island of Ponies," an illustrated story of that experience, and submitted it to *Scribner's Monthly*. Auspiciously, it was accepted.

Shortly thereafter one of the owners of Scribner's got in touch with Howard's father to urge that the young man come to New York, suggesting that a promising opportunity awaited him there. The family decided that this was a chance not to be missed, and in October 1876 Howard set out.

He left for New York full of confidence and high spirits. Fortunately, things did not go as easily as he had expected. Scribner's offered only limited support. He had to prove himself, and had a hard time making his way. He had to struggle to understand the artistic requirements and printing practicalities of the business before he could be taken on as a regular contributor to the magazines. His picture *ideas* were good, but the pictures themselves had to be redrawn by other artists to meet the graphic standards of the magazines and the discriminate requirements of the engravers who hand carved the wood blocks for the press.

Finally, after a tough year in New York, he was able, after working more than six weeks on it, to have his picture, *Wreck in the Offing*, accepted without redrawing — and, furthermore, published as a double page spread in *Harper's Weekly*. From then on his path opened up. As he gained experience, he began to build a reputation, and he was welcomed into the elite group of recognized illustrators that included Edwin Austin Abbey, Arthur B. Frost, and Charles S. Reinhart. During this period, his many letters to his mother reveal what biographer Elizabeth Nesbitt terms "Pyle himself, the romanticism which was so inherent a quality, the versatility of his imagination, the response to the spirit of folk literature, to its ways of expression, to its humour and wisdom. And always he seems to have thought of stories in terms of pictures, of the illustrations which a story or any piece of literature would inspire."[5]

Two years later in 1879, fairly well assured of assignments, especially from Harper's, and with many of his colleagues having left the city, he decided to return to Wilmington. There he planted his roots. A year and a half after his return he married (with Arthur Frost as best man) Anne Poole, a member of an old Wilmington Quaker family. By 1883 he was doing so well in his profession that he was able to build a new studio for himself near the edge of town.

For the rest of his life Howard Pyle never stopped working on drawing, painting, and writing. He produced for publication more than 3,300 illustrations, a rate of about two a week. He wrote 19 books, several of which appeared first in magazines. Additionally, for the magazines, he produced 80 or so illustrated stories, poems, and essays. Thirteen of his books were written and illustrated for children and young people.

He knew fulfillment in his career. In 1897 he reflected:

If the word "illustrator" be etymologically defined, how proud should he be of having brought his light into the darkness; how should he glory in having illuminated the pages of literature with reflected fragments of God's wholesome sunlight as it shines upon the world of created things.[6]

(cat. 8) **The Last Leaf,** *1892*

(cat. 10) **Along the Canal in Old Manhattan**, *1893*

19

(cat. 11) ***The Death of Braddock****, 1893*

(cat. 12) ***A Night in the Village Street***, *1893*

(cat. 13) *He Had Found the Captain Agreeable and Companionable*, 1894

Also in those years of work Pyle gained a reputation as an esteemed teacher of illustration. He was motivated by the same inducements that motivate any good teacher — belief in the fundamental value of the subject and a desire to help others, in this case down a path he himself had trod. He was a great teacher. Most of the succeeding generation's best illustrators were products of his school. And a number of those students then taught, using Pyle's tenets, many of the better illustrators that succeeded them.

Though Pyle possessed abundant technical facility he did not teach technique; he taught instead how to express thought, feeling, emotion. Throughout his teaching career his teaching principles remained the same, but there was nothing static about his approach; it evolved through a number of phases. He began in 1894 by accepting an offer to teach an illustration class for one half day a week at the recently opened Drexel Institute of Art, Science, and Industry in Philadelphia. He had thirty-nine students that first year. By the end of the next academic year his class was nationally known — exemplified by the achievements of such students as Violet Oakley, Maxfield Parrish, Jesse Willcox Smith, and Elizabeth Shippen Green. Thereupon Drexel established The School of Illustration, and Pyle commuted to Philadelphia for two full days of teaching a week.

Then, in 1898, to concentrate on the best of his pupils and maintain their progress during Drexel's vacation period, he invited the ten most promising to participate in special summer classes in the village of Chadds Ford, Pennsylvania, twelve miles from Wilmington. This summer school continued through 1903. Its participants, throughout their lives, carried with them fond memories of the pleasure and stimulation of those summer weeks at Chadds Ford with Pyle and his wife and six children. Howard Pyle's students loved him. They never forgot him.

(cat. 14) *A Reminiscence of the Marigold*, 1894

(cat. 15) *"Speak up, Boy, — Speak up," Said the Gentleman*, 1894

(cat. 16) ***The Trotting Match****, 1894*

(cat. 17) ***The Admiral Came in His Gig of State,*** *1895*

(cat. 18) **The Constitution's** *Last Fight, 1895*

(cat. 19) **The Pirates Fire upon the Fugitives,** *1895*

He had begun to feel, however, that a significant part of his time and energy was being wasted at Drexel. The classes were too large, only a few could really profit from his instruction, and if he were to concentrate on those few it would be unfair to the others. He devised a new plan — to build a studio next to his own for selected students who could profit from his intensive, specialized instruction. So in 1900 he resigned from Drexel, and then, from many applicants, invited twelve students, some of whom had been at Drexel, to enroll in the Howard Pyle School of Art in Wilmington. This new plan met with immediate success. The school became famous; by 1903 several hundred applications were received of which only three could be accepted.

In addition to the individual advice and criticism he gave each student, the heart of his teaching in Wilmington was manifest in the weekly evening composition class, complemented by occasional meetings of the evening sketch club. Of his first experience with the composition class, N.C. Wyeth wrote his parents back in Needham, Massachusetts: "The composition class lasted two hours, and it opened my eyes more than any talk I ever heard. It makes [Eric] Pape look shallow."[7] Pyle was unorthodox and provocative. He put the emphasis on creation. His remarks in this class, as recorded by four of his students — Allen Tupper True, Ethel Pennewill Brown, Olive Rush, and Charles DeFeo — reveal his conception of art and illustration:

I criticize these compositions by analysis but an illustration cannot be made that way — it must be made by inspiration.
If you *live* in a picture the drawing will be good.[8]

All great art is the expression of some great truth. *Tell the limpid truth.* The great works of art are great because they tell the truth, simply and directly.
Let your soul flow into your picture.
The Painter [must] touch the universal in his subject.
Art is not a transcript of nature nor a copy. Art is the expression of those beauties and emotions that stir the human soul.[9]

And to stress the critical importance of concentrated effort when first laying in the composition of a picture: "After the first half-hour of work, your lay-in should kill at a hundred yards."[10]

The evening sketch club was both fun and a challenge to the imagination. Each time, one of the students took his or her turn as host and assigned a theme, such as *The End, Idiocy, The Conqueror*, and everyone would draw his or her own idea of that theme. Pyle participated, not as a master but as a member. After an hour the sketches were exhibited and evaluated by the group. The one acclaimed the best earned its maker the gift of Pyle's signed sketch. The other sketches were given numbers and distributed by lot.

Pyle's success as a teacher stemmed not just from his philosophy of art, but from the warm yet powerful way in which he dealt with his students. As Maxfield Parrish later recalled: "It was not so much the actual things he taught us as contact with his personality that really counted. Somehow after a talk with him you felt inspired to go out and do great things, and wondered afterwards by what magic he did it."[11] And N.C. Wyeth wrote in April 1904: "Mr. Pyle is at the bottom of my present standing, and

(cat. 20) ***She is Drunk. It Will Soon Pass Away***

(Some of the By-Standers Said: "She is Drunk. It Will Soon Pass Away"), *1895*

*(cat. 21) **The Surrender of Captain Pearson** (**The Surrender of Captain Pearson On the Deck of the** Bon Homme Richard), 1895*

(cat. 22) **We Escaped in the Boat***, 1895*

(cat. 23) ***The Champlain Tows**, 1896*

without him I'd have missed the *biggest* part of my life, and *the thing* is something I can't explain."[12]

By the middle of the decade, the structure of the group receiving his guidance was undergoing change, moving from young students just starting out on an illustration career to an older group. This older group was made up of graduates of his school, like Frank Schoonover, George Harding, and W.J. Aylward, along with newly arrived professionals who had moved to Wilmington to be near him and benefit from his advice and criticism — artists like Anton Otto Fischer, Harold M. Brett, and John Wolcott Adams.

Over the years, Pyle taught more than a hundred artists. As a measure of his commitment, he never charged tuition for his teaching. But he had his reward. As early as 1896 he told James MacAlister, President of Drexel, "I know of no better legacy a man can leave to the world than that he had aided others to labor at an art so beautiful as that to which I have devoted my life."[13] And in 1897: "there is a singular delight in beholding the lucid thoughts of a pupil growing into form and color."[14] Furthermore, his teaching probably benefited him as well as his students — he could evaluate his own performance in relation to what he was teaching, and he may well have gotten new

(cat. 28) **Leisurely Drifting through Farm Lands**, *1896*

(cat. 32) **Wide Damp Reaches of Brightness**, *1896*

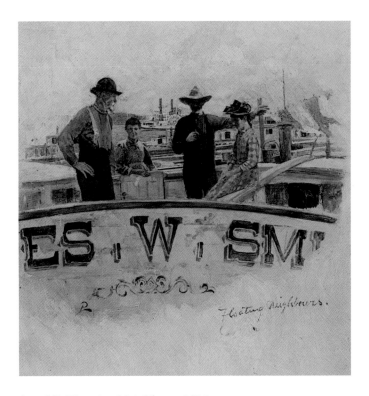

(cat. 25) *Floating Neighbors*, 1896

ideas from observing the varied talents of his better students — N.C. Wyeth or Harvey Dunn, for example.

At the turn of the century he became interested in mural painting, which was growing in demand as decoration for the many new public buildings in the country. It seemed a fruitful way of applying his vast and detailed knowledge of American history and his skill in illustration. After executing three mural commissions between 1905 and 1910 he decided to devote himself to that field, and to do so he felt the need to learn from the early Italian masters. In November 1910 he took his family to Italy for an extended stay. He was deeply impressed by the work of the Italian painters. After a year, however, his health failed. In November 1911, at the age of 58 and at the height of his powers, he died and was buried in Florence.

So we have answered the first question posed near the beginning of this essay: What fashioned Howard Pyle's inspiration and how did he build his career? But what about the second question? Has his concept of a brilliant future for book illustration been fulfilled? The answer has to be that while illustration is today a vibrant force in publishing, it has not as yet been "uplifted into that higher plane of excellence" that Howard Pyle envisaged.

In today's world of illustration we are seeing the results of the great technological advances in photography and reproduction that began during Howard Pyle's time. The sheer quantity of book and magazine pictures has increased many fold. Pictures now come "cheap and easy" — they are commonplace. Just look at a magazine stand — dozens of magazines, most with half or more of their space occupied by colored pictures. With representational pictures this commonplace, can one wonder at the critical success of non-representational painting? Is not the assemblage of little cubes and the application of paint dribbles and the

(cat. 26) *The Floating Water Home*, 1896

(cat. 30) **These Little Gardens**, *1896*

(cat. 31) **Vignette** *(woman on a houseboat), 1896*

*(cat. 27) Headpiece for **The Romance of an Ambrotype**, 1896*

*(cat. 29) Tailpiece for **The Romance of an Ambrotype**, 1896*

*(cat. 24) **The Convalescent**, 1896*

(cat. 33) **The Mizzentop of the Redoubtable,** *1897*

(cat. 45) **The Lighters Were Soon Alongside**, *1907*

drawing of soup cans a reaction, in part, to the plethora of representational pictures? Épatez la bourgeoisie!

At the same time the nature of book illustration has changed. With much illustrated adult non-fiction, for example the typical parlor table book, the pictures are not the product of today's "patient draughtsman." Original drawing and painting has been largely displaced by photographs, accompanied by occasional use of artwork from the past (often cropped to suit and with no credit given). For those non-fiction books that are primarily text, such as history, biography, travel, the few photographs are used not to decorate but to elucidate the text, and usually not even used effectively for that purpose. To save a few cents the photographs are crammed together at one or two spots in the book rather than being located appropriately in relation to the text.

For adult fiction, illustration prospered when pictures were scarce and publication in fiction magazines and books provided one of the best opportunities for many people to view pictures. Today such books are seldom illustrated at all, except for the hardcover dust jacket or the front cover of the paperback. There are well designed front covers, but for books like the high volume "romance" fiction paperback, you know the formula — raised gilt lettering; the man: bare chest, muscles; the woman: buxom, décolletage — the picture serves the seller, not the reader.

At any rate, illustration of serious adult fiction is often problematic and always has been. An illustration for a novel or short story may intrude upon the author's right to use words, with all their subtleties and complexities, in setting the scenes and characterizing the people. The illustrator must put his own interpretation upon the scenes and people, and while it may be a great and even an inspired interpretation, it is necessarily a somewhat different interpretation from the author's unless author and artist are the same person. Much of the best fiction does not need illustration; in fact it often cannot be satisfactorily illustrated. And many authors may not want their work illustrated by another mind.

For children's books, however, drawn or painted illustration is just as essential as it was in Pyle's day. Pictures are highly important for children — well worth a thousand words, especially if they don't understand 800 of them. First graders know 6,000 words, adults 30,000 or more. To catch and hold their attention, as well as to serve their comprehension and imagination, children's books must have pictures. The result is that children's book illustration is alive and flourishing, working with the words to provide visual experience and stories they can depict in their minds.

Of course, depending upon the setting and the skill of the artist, a drawn or painted picture, with its visualization of thought and its own innate aesthetic, can also be worth many words to an adult, sometimes well over a thousand. This is obviously true for caricature. Al Hirschfeld, epitomizing the previous night's theater performance with beauty of line and an understanding of human connections, is the twentieth century counterpart of Thomas Nast on nineteenth century politics. And for functional books, such as bird guides, the low cost and high reproduction quality provided by today's technology has made possible the creation of lovely and useful tools. The hundreds of paintings in a bird guide are essential to its function, a function that cannot be carried out effectively by photography. Only the painting has the ability to present the distinguishing features while minimizing extraneous and confusing details.

The comic strip is a lively force in today's publishing business. A good deal of it may be of dubious quality, but

(cat. 49) **'Tween Decks of the Slaver**, *1907*

(cat. 34) **Nelson At the Battle of Copenhagen (Nelson Sealing the Letter to the Crown Prince of Denmark at the Battle of Copenhagen)**, *1897*

(cat. 48) **The Rest Were Shot and Thrown Overboard**, *1907*

*(cat. 60) Title page for **The Salem Wolf**, 1909*

*(cat. 57) Marginal illustration for **The Salem Wolf**, 1909*

that is true for any form of entertainment or "art." Some, for example *Calvin and Hobbes*, or *The Far Side*, display intriguing wit and skill. Finally, fantasy and science fiction, areas in which photography is not possible, are also attracting artists and illustrators.

So illustration, broadly considered, is essential for many purposes and is today a practical and commercial success. But what of its artistic growth? Can we predict whether Pyle's hope will eventually be fulfilled, that "the art of beautifying books with pictures shall . . . be uplifted into a higher and a different plane of excellence?" To answer that, the critical questions would seem to be, "Is the fine illustrated book, with all its potential for beauty and harmony, basically a sound idea? Does it have intrinsic artistic value? Is it something people want and will be willing to pay for?" I believe that the answer to all three of those questions is "Yes."

The illustrated books and magazines of a century ago, with their specially drawn pictures, sometimes with decorated initial letters, headpieces, tailpieces, and marginal vignettes, trace their tradition back to the illuminated manuscripts of the Middle Ages and early Renaissance. People's love for books has existed for hundreds of years. It still exists. The Morgan Library's recent exhibit of 96 illuminated Books of Hours was, according to a library spokesperson, "tremendously well received by the press and the public and achieved one of our highest attendances ever."[15] The popular love of books does not seem to have been extinguished by television, movies, and the World Wide Web.

Many millions of books are bought every year around the world, and sales figures show that interest in books in the United States has been growing. If even a small fraction of the market were devoted to beautiful illustrated books, that would fulfill Howard Pyle's vision. And there is today (and doubtless will continue to be) no lack of skillful artists who ardently want to pursue a career in book illustration.

So, in the longer run, while a clear route to it may not be apparent today, there is a good chance that Howard Pyle's concept will be realized — that some years hence, distinguished books, alluringly embellished with original

illustration designed specially for them, will enter successfully into the marketplace and be regarded as precious
possessions. The best of them will necessarily be high
priced. But they will also be highly valued.

But the immediate interest of those reading this catalogue or attending this exhibit is not, of course, the future
of book illustration. It is the quality of Howard Pyle's pictures and the pleasure and satisfaction to be gotten from
viewing the reproductions in this catalogue and the originals on the walls of the museum — separated from their
texts. This brings us to our final question: What makes
Howard Pyle's pictures effective as book illustrations and
why put an exhibit of pictures meant for books on the
walls of an art gallery?

There is an easy answer to the second part of that question. Viewing the reproduction in its book and the original
on the wall are two different experiences — and each has
its own special value. A picture designed to illustrate and
decorate a text collaborates in the composite meaning and
decor when seen in its home within the book. On the other
hand there are aspects in the texture, scope, and isolation of
an original that cannot be apparent in the reproduction.

While a few of the pictures in this collection were
painted by Pyle with no thought of publication, most were
made to be viewed as reproductions on a page in relation
to their text. But the viewer will find, I am confident, a
great deal of satisfaction in seeing them both on the walls
of the Brandywine River Museum and reproduced in this
catalogue. They can stand eloquently alone, independent
of their text.

Elizabeth Nesbitt, in her short monograph on
Howard Pyle, described her experience on first viewing
Pyle's pictures in the flesh — the originals on the walls of
the Delaware Art Museum:

(cat. 58) Marginal illustration for
***The Salem Wolf**, 1909*

(cat. 56) Marginal illustration for
The Salem Wolf, *1909*

The illustrations are dramatic, romantic, striking in their color . . . magnificent, strong in character portrayal, imaginative in story-telling quality, vigorous, forceful, and compelling. One look at some of the originals, [however], shows that the reproductions, impressive as they are, do not do justice to the scope of the pictures, to the intense color, to the fineness of detail, to the entire conceptions of the pictures. One look is unsatisfactory; to many of them one is drawn a second and a third time, and it is difficult to select those which most deserve comment.[16]

Now, what of the other part of our third question? What makes Howard Pyle's pictures effective as book illustrations, as reproductions in a catalogue, and as Elizabeth Nesbitt found, also highly effective as wall pictures. Some of the best witnesses for their value in books should be the authors whose works he illustrated. For example, in November 1906 author Basil King wrote to Pyle:

> Permit me to thank you for the beautiful illustrations with which you have enobled — the word is just — my little story of Mary Dyer, in the November issue of *McClure's*. I cannot but feel that if I had only seen the illustrations first, I should have written a better tale.[17]

And in 1896 Woodrow Wilson wrote in connection with his series on George Washington that appeared in *Harper's New Monthly Magazine*:

> I must write at once to express my admiration for the illustrations you have made for my first article. They seem to me in every way admirable. They heighten

(cat. 62) *The Wolf and Dr. Wilkinson (Once it Chased Doctor Wilkinson Into the Very Town Itself)*, 1909

(cat. 63) Marginal illustration for
Ysobel de Corveaux, *1910*

(cat. 64) Marginal illustration for
Ysobel de Corveaux, *1910*

the significance of the text, not only being entirely in its spirit, but are themselves besides, perfect in their kind. The last of the three seems to me especially delightful for its human truth.[18]

Pyle earned this kind of approbation by bringing to his picture making all those talents of hand, mind, and heart acquired over years of dedicated effort. He had the ability to organize a picture so that while each element is interesting in itself all elements as a whole serve the essential purpose of the picture. As he wrote to Henry Cabot Lodge, the author of the 1897 *Story of the Revolution*, which Pyle had illustrated:

> Pictorial art must represent some salient point that shall convey as in a whole view a certain given situation. It shall not require any text to explain it, but should explain itself and all the circumstances belonging to it.[19]

The Shell demonstrates this. The picture does not describe a specific incident in the text, but instead strikingly typifies the general situation in Vicksburg at the time of its siege. And for *Vitia and the Governor*, Howard Pyle used to evoke that scene just a single line of the text "She must have been, at the time she murdered the governor, not quite twenty." That is the only direct mention of the murder in the entire story.

Take note as you view these pictures of the thought and care Pyle used in constructing his compositions. You can feel the power with which he adroitly brings you into each picture — even viewed from a distance you are often lured in. For this he used a variety of methods, in each case the one best suited to the subject. As art historian Deane Keller has particularized:

Pyle used the essential constituents of composition authoritatively. His use of balance, line interrelationship, scale proportion, focal centers, light and dark patterns, repetitions of sharpest lines, rhythms, variations, counters and the rest was masterly. He controlled the flat two-dimensional style, exhibited in many of the pen-and-ink pieces as well as the three-dimensional.[20]

Pyle was fearless about placing the viewer in the most spectacular position to see his action scenes. He pulls you right into that action, regardless of whether it violates pictorial convention. He has you between the two careening frigates in *The **Constitution's** Last Fight*; looking up from the deck below at the snipers in *The Mizzentop of the **Redoubtable*** who shot and killed Nelson at the Battle of Trafalgar; in the forefront of the Confederate line, bearing the brunt of *The Charge* of the Union cavalry. In his quieter scenes he positions the viewer more subtly but with equal thought and care. You are in that meadow *In the Valley of Delight* along with the King and the ladies of the golden hair; and pondering with *Roger Bacon* in his cell while the women worry in the background; and spending a quiet evening on the path *Along the Canal in Old Manhattan*.

There are many black and white oils in this collection. Pyle was a master of this en grisaille work, enforced by the near absence of color reproduction in his earlier illustration years. And true artistry by no means requires color. (That is certainly so for photography. Ansel Adams, one of our greatest photographic artists, did not need color; did not want it.) And in painting, grisaille has its advantages — light and shade seem to come through more clearly. Notice how essential both to the composition and the meaning of the scene is the moonlit smoke produced by grisaille in *The **Constitution's** Last Fight*.

(cat. 65) ***The Prisoner****, 1910*

Howard Pyle said, notably, that the artist must *live* in the picture. But for true understanding and enjoyment, so too must the viewer. And lack of color is the least of the problems for the suspension of disbelief required for living in a picture. Color is not essential to that suspension — when looking at a movie you soon forget that it's not real; if it's a black and white movie, you forget just as quickly that it's not in Technicolor. Just lose yourself in the picture — you will *feel* color in Howard Pyle's black and whites.

A similar principle applies to a picture's frame. On first viewing, an attractive and appropriate frame is an important part of the mise en scène; it helps put you in the mood. But a picture lives *inside* its frame — if *you* live in it too, your mind soon obliterates whatever is outside the picture itself.

Pyle also excelled in pen and ink drawing, which he deployed in a number of widely different styles to suit the subject. He used pen and ink extensively in illustrating his children's books and for decoration of other stories and poems. A number of his drawings are in this collection.

He used light effectively, in both color and black and white pictures, particularly in his night scenes. Notice how in *Vitia and the Governor* he has brought the blue moonglow and the orange lamplight in from the two different directions, and how he has handled the lamplight in *The Passing of Doña Victoria* and the reflected candlelight in *She Saw Herself for What He Had Said*. His use of moonlight has dramatically fortified the composition of *The Haunted House*. Pyle's moons are superb: look at the variety of provocative moons in *Henry V, Gallows Point, Along the Canal in Old Manhattan*, and *The Wolf and Dr. Wilkinson*.

Nor did Pyle overlook the pictorial opportunities in his handling of daylight — the subtly varying color of the sky and the water in *The Wreck*, the compositional use of the bits of bright sunlight in *A Dream of Young Summer*, and

(cat. 59) **She Saw Herself for What He Had Said, and Swooned**, *1909*

(cat. 67) Head of a Woman, undated

the dramatic contrast between *The Shell*'s gloomy foreground and its sunlit fragment of distant landscape.

Beyond all these skills in composition and in handling of light and color and line, Pyle succeeded by following the advice he gave his students:

> a man is not an artist by virtue of clever technique or brilliant methods: he is fundamentally an artist in the degree that he is able to sense and appreciate the significance of life that surrounds him, and to express that significance to the minds of others.[21]

Howard Pyle had that sense and appreciation — had a deep understanding of how people feel and how to make a picture express that feeling. In *The Last Leaf*, just the posture of the man leads you to imagining all you need to know about what he is feeling. Likewise, you can sense the woman's foreboding in *The Haunted House*, the triangulated tension in *The Forest Madman*, the parasoled woman's paralyzing fear in *The Shell*, and the watchful trepidation in *The Spy*.

And Pyle powerfully created the sense of a scene: *The Charge* — impetuosity; *The Wolf and Dr. Wilkinson* — headlong flight; *Leisurely Drifting through Farm Lands* — bucolic serenity; *The Wreck* — the broad, the ungovernable, the beautiful sea.

Deane Keller also said "the range and penetration of Pyle's genius as a significant draughtsman is to be compared with that of the greatest in the field of painting — Rembrandt, Giotto, Leonardo, Daumier, Goya."[22]

Adequate praise.

Enough. I'll close with this extract from a letter that N.C. Wyeth, late in his life, wrote to his wife about their daughter-in-law, Caroline Pyle Wyeth, Howard Pyle's niece:

> Somehow, I feel that Caroline has inherited an important gift from Howard Pyle, and I have a strangely significant feeling that if I have succeeded in starting this talent toward something good, that it will give me a certain mystical satisfaction and the sense that in some degree I have perpetuated something of the spirit of my old teacher and master, who, as the years roll by, is assuming greater and greater proportions as an artist, as a man, and as my benefactor.[23]

(cat. 87) *I am Captain John Mackra ("I am Captain John Mackra," Said I, and I Sat Down upon the Gunwale of the Boat)*, 1887

(cat. 71) **Woman at a Spinning Wheel,** *1879*

(cat. 74) **Suspicious Strangers**, *1881*

(cat. 73) Study for **Suspicious Strangers**, *1881*

(cat. 76) **Endicott Cutting the Cross Out of the English Flag,** *1883*

(cat. 69) **The Little Boys Cheered Vigorously**
(The Little Boys Cheered Vigorously as
He Pushed Off), *1879*

A·VERSE·WITH·A·MORAL·BUT·NO·NAME:·

A wise man once, of Haarlem town,
Went wandering up, and wandering down,
And ever the question asked:

"If all the world was paper,
    And if all the sea was ink,
And if the trees were bread and cheese,
    What would we do for drink?"

Then all the folk, both great and small,
    Began to beat their brains,
But they could not answer him at all,
    In spite of all their pains.

But still he wandered here and there,
    That man of great renown,
And still he questioned everywhere,
    The folk of Haarlem town:

"If all the world was paper,
    And if all the sea was ink,
And if the trees were bread and cheese,
    What would we do for drink?"

Full thin he grew, as, day by day,
    He toiled with mental strain,
Until the wind blew him away,
    And he ne'er was seen again.

And now methinks I hear you say,
"Was ere a man so foolish, pray,
    Since first the world began?"
Oh, hush! I'll tell you secretly,
Down East there dwells a man, and he
Is asking questions constantly,
That none can answer, that I see;
    Yet he's a wise-wise man!

H Pyle

(cat. 77) **A Verse with a Moral but No Name**, 1884

Notes

1 Howard Pyle, "Concerning the Art of Illustration," *First Year Book of the Bibliophile Society* (Boston: Bibliophile Society, 1902), p. 21.

2 *Proceedings of the 42nd Annual Convention of the American Institute of Architects*, Glenn Brown, ed. (Washington, D.C.: Gibson Bros., 1909), p. 255.

3 Howard Pyle, "When I Was a Little Boy," *Woman's Home Companion*, 39 (April 1912):5. The article, written about 1903, was published posthumously.

4 For a description of van der Wielen's school, see Cecilia Beaux, *Background with Figures* (Boston and New York: Houghton Mifflin, 1930. She misspells the name. Bénézit and Thieme-Becker are authorities for the spelling used here.

5 Elizabeth Nesbitt, *Howard Pyle* (New York: Henry Z. Walck, 1966), p. 13.

6 Howard Pyle, "Notes on the Illustrations," in Henry Wadsworth Longfellow *Evangeline* (Boston: Houghton Mifflin, 1897), p. xiv.

7 N. C. Wyeth to his mother, November 3, 1902, in Betsy James Wyeth, ed., *The Wyeths: The Letters of N. C. Wyeth*, 1901-1945 (Boston: Gambit, 1971), p. 21. Wyeth had studied with Pape at the Eric Pape School of Art in Boston in 1901.

*(cat. 79) Headpiece for **How One turned his Trouble to some account**, 1885*

YE SONG OF YE GOSSIPS

1

One old maid,
And another old maid,
And another old maid - that's three -
And they were a gossiping, I am afraid,
As they sat sipping their tea.

2

They talked of this,
And they talked of that,
In the usual gossiping way
Until everybody was black as your hat,
And the only ones white were they.

3

One old maid,
And another old maid, -
For the third had gone into the street -
Who talked in a way of that third old maid,
Which never would do to repeat.

4

And now but one
Dame sat all alone,
For the others were both away.
"I've never yet met," said she, with a groan,
"Such scandalous talkers as they.

5

Alas! and alack!"
"We're all of a pack!
For no matter how we walk,
Or what folk say to our face, our back
Is sure to breed gossip and talk."

H. PYLE:-

(cat. 78) *Ye Song of ye Gossips*, 1884

60

 he Brave Soldier bringeth
his Trouble to ỹ town along with him.

(cat. 80) *The Brave Soldier bringeth his Trouble to ye town along with him*, 1885

(cat. 81) ***Here the Brave Soldier brings his trouble before the king to find if it shall follow him wherever he goes***, 1885

8 Allen Tupper True, "Notebook," pre-1906, as excerpted by Richard Waye Likes, circa 1947. Document in the library of the Delaware Art Museum, Wilmington.

9 Ethel Pennewill Brown and Olive Rush, "Red Books," a manuscript in which the two women "each wrote what we remembered of Mr. Pyle's talks — then we *combined* our efforts and wrote these notes" after each lecture. Document in the library of the Delaware Art Museum, Wilmington.

10 Charles DeFeo, "Personal Reminiscences of Howard Pyle," in *Diversity in Depth* (Wilmington: Delaware Art Museum, 1973), p. 17.

11 Parrish to Richard Wayne Lykes, March 1945, in Richard Wayne Lykes, "Howard Pyle, Teacher of Illustration," *Pennsylvania Magazine of History and Biography* 80, no. 4 (spring, 1945): 347. In the article, the word "afterwards" was inadvertently omitted from the quotation.

12 N. C. Wyeth to his mother, April 11, 1904, in *The Wyeths*, p. 80.

13 Charles D. Abbott, *Howard Pyle: A Chronicle* (New York & London: Harper & Bros., 1925), p. 207.

14 Pyle, "Notes on the Illustrations," p. xv.

15 Telephone conversation with an identified "anonymous spokesperson," Communications Department, Morgan Library, January 9, 1998.

16 Nesbitt, *Pyle*, p. 60.

17 As quoted in Abbott, *Pyle*, p. 170. King's story, "The Hanging of Mary Dyer," appeared in *McClure's* in November 1906.

18 Abbott, *Pyle*, p. 158. As we know, Woodrow Wilson was nothing if not critical.

19 Abbott, *Pyle*, p. 168.

20 Deane Keller, "Howard Pyle: His Contribution to the American Spirit," address given at the Delaware Art Center, April 19, 1942, p. 7. Typescript, Delaware Art Museum library, Wilmington.

21 Abbott, *Pyle*, p. 226. Pyle to W.M.R. French, July 17, 1905.

22 Keller, "Pyle," p. 7.

23 Henry C. Pitz, *Howard Pyle, Writer, Illustrator, Founder of the Brandywine School* (New York: Clarkson N. Potter, 1975) p. 225. Pitz incorrectly states that the letter was about N. C. Wyeth's daughter Carolyn.

*(cat. 82) Half-title for **Pepper and Salt**, 1886*

*(cat. 83) Headpiece for **Pepper and Salt**, 1886*

*(cat. 84) Tailpiece for **Pepper and Salt** (List of Illustrations),*

*(cat. 85) Tailpiece for **Pepper and Salt** (Preface), 1886*

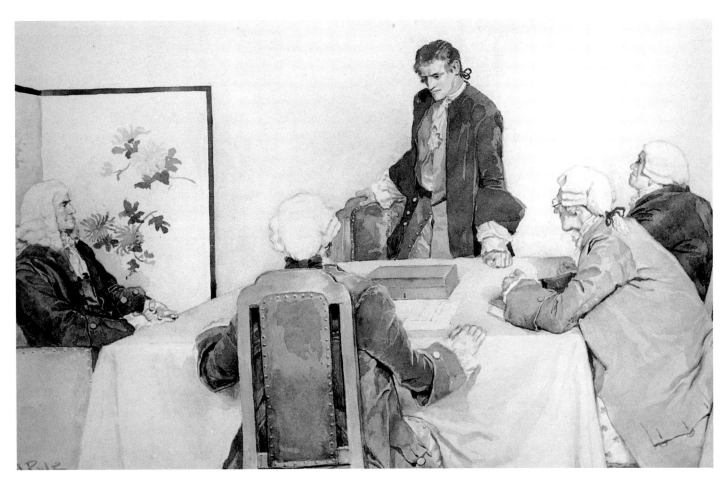

(cat. 88) **I Rose Slowly from My Chair (I Rose slowly from my Chair, and Stood with My Hand Leaning upon the Table)**, *1887*

(cat. 86) **Apollo Slaying the Python**, *1887*

(cat. 89) **Palamedes Tests the Madness of Odysseus**, *1887*

Photograph of Howard P. Brokaw on horseback, Tucson, Arizona, 1997.

How and Why We Collected
by Howard P. Brokaw

The occasion was a visit thirty-five years ago by a friend from Akron, where Dede and I had lived just before our recent return to Delaware. Betsy Wyeth was the friend's cousin so we drove the ten miles up the Brandywine to see Betsy and Andy. Sitting around chatting, Andy suddenly asked me, "Howard, do you collect your grandfather's pictures?" I answered, "No." Andy looked me straight in the eye and said just two words, "You should."

It was an epiphany. The intensity in his voice struck home; immediately I knew he was right.

Our Howard Pyle collection dates from that moment. (We might have started earlier if I'd listened to my wife.) We did have at the time a few Pyle pictures and a few books, accumulated through no effort on our part. Thirty years earlier my grandmother Anne Pyle had given me two drawings from the King Arthur series. My mother, Phoebe Pyle Brokaw, had sent me the three small paintings from the "Cruise of the Caribbee" to hang in my room at Princeton, and had given us *The Passing of Doña Victoria* for an engagement present. And in 1950 Dede's mother had bought us *The Spy* from a friend in Easton, Maryland — for $70. Neither the owner nor her daughter wanted it; they just wanted to be rid of it.

But after Andy Wyeth's signal exhortation, which I'm sure he doesn't remember (I'll ask him next time I see him), we began to collect. A long time before this, Gertrude Brincklé, Howard Pyle's secretary, had given us a copy of the Morse and Brincklé bibliography of Pyle's pictures and

(cat. 92) ***Decorative Initial I***, *1890*

69

(cat. 94) **Gallows Point**, *1890*

(cat. 98) **Village scene in Jamaica***, 1890*

writings. I hadn't paid attention to it. Now I began to study it. Entranced, I submerged myself in it, reading every word. At about that same time the Studio Group, an organization of women artists who owned and used the Howard Pyle studio, put on a show of privately held Pyle pictures, including our few. What we saw at that show quickened our collecting urge.

Our first addition to the collection occurred in early 1964. My parents had owned a few Pyle pictures and as my siblings and I divided up the household goods from our father's estate, I chose, whenever I could, the Pyle pictures instead of other items. We ended up with eight pictures including *Suspicious Strangers* and *Henry V at Agincourt* (we call that one Hank Cinq).

Then in early 1965, came our first opportunity to buy a picture. At that time the Delaware Art Museum was not in the market for Pyle pictures, so when *On the Way to Tyburn* was offered to them by William MacPherson, a dealer in Boston, the museum's curator, Roland Elzea, kindly called me. In our then somewhat straightened circumstances, it was fortunate that the price seemed affordable — $150. This was followed in later years by three others through MacPherson, *Quo Vadis, Domine, Endicott Cutting the Cross out of the English Flag*, and *Recruiting for the Mexican War*.

Two other great opportunities surfaced in 1965. We bought from my Aunt Martha, Godfrey Pyle's widow, five

(cat. 93) **Executing an Intricate Passage***, 1890*

(cat. 90) **The Prince Pours Water into the Barrel**, *1888*

(cat. 91) **The Two Thieves**, *1889*

*(cat. 95) **He Met a Poor Woman Coming Home from the Market**, 1890*

*(cat. 96) **It Was a Very Gay Dinner**, 1890*

(cat. 97) ***The King and the Beggar Feasted***, *1890*

(cat. 102) **He Called the Wisest Men of the Island to Him**, 1891

*(cat. 104) Title page for **The Enchanted Island**, 1891*

*(cat. 105) **The Deacon's Masterpiece: or, the Wonderful "One-Hoss-Shay"**, 1892*

(cat. 100) **Along the Highway Furiously**, *1891*

(cat. 101) Alternate tailpiece for
Peter Rugg Ye Bostonian, *1891*

(cat. 103) **He Came to the Cross-roads and the Stone Cross**, *1891*

pictures, including *The Wreck* and three King Arthur drawings. Then the best deal we ever made came about. Through the Bartfield Gallery on New York's West 57th Street, we learned of a collector in north Jersey who was tired of his Pyles and wanted to switch his collecting to musical instruments. We drove up there and bought thirteen pictures, including *The Wolf and Dr. Wilkinson, The Shell*, and *I Am Captain John Mackra*. I didn't have the money for this deal; had to float a loan at the bank before we left. I laid down the offer in cash — I'd learned that the sight of green is far more enticing than words or a check.

With each new acquisition our appetite grew. We finished off the year in December with the six small paintings for "Through Inland Waters." Most of the other pictures from this story are owned by the Library of Congress. We got ours from Kennedy Galleries, where we had purchased *Roger Bacon* earlier in the year. Kennedy had bought *Roger Bacon* from Washington University in St. Louis. It had been given to them by William Bixby, who had bought it and the other four Bibliophile Society paintings from Howard Pyle.

We never had another year like 1965. It was wonderful. Whenever I began to lose my nerve that year, thinking of such irrelevancies as future college expenses, I was always urged on by our son Jeffrey, aged fourteen at the time. But by the end of 1965 we'd sopped up most of the loose ones lying around. The next biggest year was 1967 with five pictures from the Sybil and Lew Munson collection, including the original oil for Pyle's bookplate. However, we kept on looking and asking, and except for the two dry years of 1982 and 1984, added more to the picture collection every year though 1988. After that, while we kept on buying as we could, the frequency of our

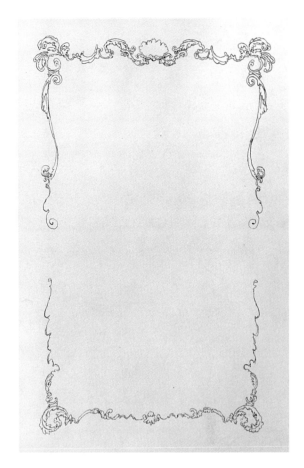

(cat. 106) Decorative border for **Dorothy Q**, *1892*

(cat. 107) **The Demon Leaped from the Earth**, *1892*

(cat. 108) **"I Think Everybody Has Gone Mad," Said the Young Man**, *1892*

(cat. 109) **Prescott on the Rampart**, 1893

ability to do so tapered off — Pyle's pictures became scarcer and exponentially higher priced.

For one reason in addition to its quality, *The Shell* was a particularly satisfying purchase. As a boy, eating my breakfast cereal in my grandmother Pyle's dining room on West 17th Street in Wilmington, I devoured, along with the cereal, two pictures, both charged with raw action and suspense — *The Shell* and *Then the Real Fight Began*. Now we owned one of them. The other I had seen being taken away sometime after my grandmother's death in 1939, bought from my Uncle Ted for $600 by a gravestone maker whose name I didn't remember. Twenty-five years went by. One day in the fall of 1966, our son Tom and I after an early morning duck hunt downstate at Red Mill Pond, stopped on the way home in Milford, Delaware to see Bill Sipple, a Delaware clock enthusiast, about a Kinkaid grandfather clock that had come down to us from Howard Pyle. We walked in to talk clocks, and there on the wall of this gravestone maker hung, to our astonishment, *Then the Real Fight Began*. Sixteen more years went by. Then, in May 1983, Bill called. He was moving into a smaller place and offered to sell us the picture. Did we snap that one up!

It was May of 1967 before I discovered Helen (Teri) Card, the first dealer to fully appreciate Howard Pyle's quality. By that time she had sold all the many pictures in her undated catalog of about 1962 — except one. When she met me at the Lebanon, New Hampshire airport, across the Connecticut River from her home in Vermont, right there in the parking lot she presented me with *'Tis Enough to Make us Both Rich Men*. She hadn't sold it because it had been torn in half and mended with what was by then discolored Scotch tape. Today, Ann Clapp having restored it, you'd never think it had been damaged. We also got from Teri Card three copper plates, a linecut, and

(cat. 110) **They are Baffled, Not Defeated**, 1893

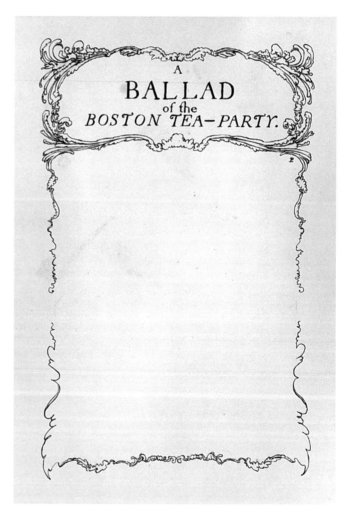

(cat. 111) *Title page for* **A Ballad of the Boston Tea-Party**, *1893*

(cat. 112) ***Melancholia****, 1895*

(cat. 113) Untitled (angel playing a flute), 1895

(cat. 114) *'Tis Enough to Make Both Rich Men*, 1896

(cat. 115) Headpiece for **Fay Song**, 1900

(cat. 116) **The Old Man**, *1902*

thirty-five woodblocks of Pyle paintings. Best of all, we bought the eight volumes of an invaluable, beautifully bound, assemblage of all Pyle's contributions to four magazines — *Harper's, Scribner's, Century*, and *St Nicholas*.

Our greatest return on the dollar was accomplished in October 1967. At an auction on the Philadelphia Pike, Dede discovered *The Passing of Sir Gawaine* buried in a lot of six other seemingly worthless pictures. The lot opened at $10 and before we could bid the auctioneer had dropped it to $5, where our son Tom and I bravely moved in for the kill — no opposition. On the way out I noticed in the room H.B. duPont, who was interested in pictures and, I suspect, may have had the wherewithal to outbid me. When we got home, Dede's mother identified one of the other six pictures — it was a lovely pastel of H.B.'s mother. She gave it to him the next day.

We bought pictures from four people connected to Howard Pyle's students. Henry Pitz's widow, Molly, sold us *Excalibur the Sword*. Henry had studied with four of Pyle's students — Harvey Dunn, Thornton Oakley, George Harding, and Walter Everett. Frank Schoonover's son, Pat, came in twice with attractive small drawings and paintings. George Harding, Jr., sold us *The Prince Pours Water into the Barrel*, and Bertha Corson Day's daughter, Bertha Cole, traded us a sketch, two small drawings, and a vignette from "The Salem Wolf" for some Pyle books selected to round out a collection she was giving to the Brandywine River Museum.

In May 1971 we had two interesting encounters. On a visit with Andy Wyeth he gave me the name of a woman in England, Pauline Ridley, who wanted to sell *The* **Constitution's** *Last Fight*. Over the telephone with her I found that the picture was in the hands of her daughter near Westerly, Rhode Island. On the way to visit Jeffrey at

 # xcalibur the Sword.

*(cat. 117) **Excalibur the Sword**, 1903*

 n the Valley of Delight

(cat. 118) *In the Valley of Delight*, 1903

he Lady Yvette the Fair.

(cat. 119) **The Lady Yvette the Fair**, 1903

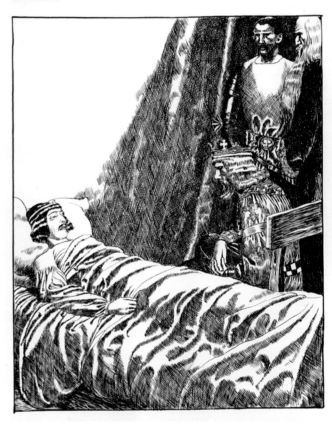

(cat. 129) **The Passing of Sir Gawaine**, 1910

The White Champion meets two Knights at the Mill.

(cat. 121) The White Champion meets two Knights at the Mill, 1903

(cat. 121) *The portrait of a young gentleman who always says "Thank you!"* 1904

Harvard, we stopped by to pick it up. We took it rather reluctantly because of an unexpected problem — peeling paint at the top because of water exposure. But Mrs. Ridley split Timothy Jayne's restoration cost with us, and the picture looks great today. In that same month, Leroy Phillips of Laurel, Delaware offered us the three drawings for "How One turned his Trouble to some account." He'd bought them at an auction of useless materials being "deaccessioned" by a library in Wilmington. He paid, for the three of them, $15. We hot-footed it down to Laurel and gave him 50 times what he'd paid. A bargain at that.

Near the end of May the following year, on the afternoon before the whole family's departure for a seven and a half week trip to Peru — balsa log rafting down the upper Amazon, backpacking over the Andes, and camping in the coastal desert — there came a notice that *The Charge* was shortly to be auctioned at Sotheby's in Los Angeles. All I could do was hurriedly call and place a bid. When we got back and opened our backlog mountain of mail, there was Sotheby's demand for prompt payment.

In August 1974 and December 1975 we bought two oils that Pyle had given to artist friends: from Childs Gallery in Boston, *A Dream of Young Summer* inscribed "To Augustus St. Gaudens this picture of Young Summer with the Fraternal Greetings of his Brother in Art: H. Pyle," and at a Sotheby's auction, *The Haunted House* inscribed to Cass Gilbert, the architect for the Woolworth Building.

Through those years, with the encouragement of all four of our children, we were also gathering, in addition to pictures, everything we could lay our hands on that had to do with Howard Pyle — particularly the books and magazines where his work had been published and any of the written ephemera of the period about Pyle. Our son, Nick, and our daughter, Chloe, had long been fascinated with

King Mark of Cornwall :·

(cat. 123) ***King Mark of Cornwall***, *1905*

ir Launcelot takes the
armor of Sir Kay.

(cat. 124) ***Sir Launcelot takes the armor of Sir Kay,*** *1905*

*(cat. 125) Tailpiece for **The Story of the Champions of the Round Table**, 1905*

Howard Pyle's writing as well as his pictures. Ultimately Gertrude Brincklé gave us her collection of Pyle books, several of them inscribed with lovely drawings by him. We found interesting documents, such as a catalogue for a 1912 Philadelphia auction of 552 items that Pyle had used as models in his paintings. Included were furniture, costumes, weapons, household goods — dating over several centuries. Another find was a catalogue for an auction in New York in 1917 of 82 of Pyle's original drawings.

Finally — and I can use that word because this began just two weeks ago — we had a call from our long time friend Murton Carpenter. She said, "I have a picture I've been meaning to give you for years. Can you and Dede come over for a drink?" Of course we could. Over a Martini we enthusiastically accepted an exciting unpublished watercolor by Howard Pyle that Murton had received as a wedding present. We dubbed it *The Escape*. Two weeks later — as I sat here writing this — Murton called after checking her wedding present list. The giver was my mother.

Everyone to some degree has the collecting urge. Andy Wyeth struck the spark that ignited the fire; fortunately the fuel was there. Collecting Howard Pyle's pictures, writings, and associated items had great appeal for us. In addition to the family relationship, there were the aesthetic and intellectual aspects of such a collection. We were after anything that could contribute to an understanding of Howard Pyle's life, thought, and work. There was variety and depth in collateral items — letters showing his relationship with other writers and artists of his time, criticism, news reports, and surprising things that would turn up that you never knew existed. Once we found a clay pipe on which he had drawn a picture. Then, adding interest to the project, was the conservation, restoration, framing, and display of our Pyle pictures. And, of course, it had its practical side. We could get started at affordable prices — a couple of orders of magnitude lower than today's. In the 1960s, Pyle was not taken seriously by art critics or dealers. The establishment of the Brandywine River Museum

The Forest Madman saveth ẏ Life of King Arthur: ⅋ ⅋

(cat. 126) **The Forest Madman saveth ye Life of King Arthur**, *1907*

Sir Geraint and the Knight of the Sparrow-hawk

(cat. 130) **Sir Geraint and the Knight of the Sparrow-hawk,** *1910*

(cat. 132) **The Escape**, *undated*

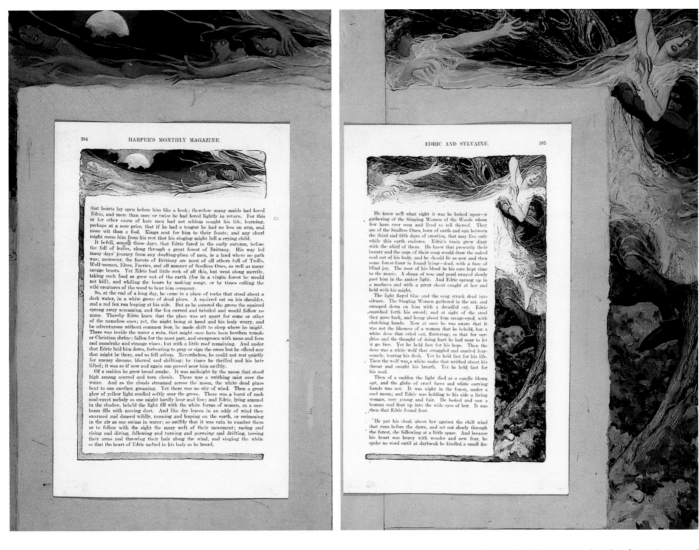

(cat. 50) Illustrative border for
Edric and Sylvaine, 1908

(cat. 51) Illustrative border for **Edric and Sylvaine**, 1908

(cat. 120) **Sea Battle between Two Frigates**, 1903

in 1971 and its exhibits over the years have had a great deal to do with today's recognition of Howard Pyle.

Then, just a year ago, in February 1997, came a second epiphany. I attended a board meeting of the RARE Center for Tropical Conservation down near the tip of Baja California. Accommodations were scarce at this isolated, rather wild area, so I roomed with David Hill, a FedEx airplane captain and founder of RARE who had seen our Pyle collection when he once stayed with us. Not long into this three day event, Dave suddenly asked me, "Howard, what are you planning for your Howard Pyle collection? Is it to be broken up at your death?" Just as Andy Wyeth's exhortation had done, this question hit hard. It revealed to me my failure to face the need to reach and make a wise decision. We needed to take action.

Once exposed to this revelation, the best course was not difficult for Dede and me to determine. We had often observed the fate of a hard won collection at the death of the couple who had built it. By design or necessity it would often end up at auction. If the collection was not rare and was reproducible this wasn't necessarily a bad thing, particularly for other collectors. But we had always thought it sad when such a collection could never or only with great difficulty be replicated. This, we thought, was the case with ours.

The decision on where to put it was even easier. Where else but the Brandywine Conservancy and its Brandywine River Museum? Frolic Weymouth, its founder, was the person who was superbly celebrating the Brandywine School, which Howard Pyle had started. I also had a sneaking suspicion that Frolic might be interested in our pictures. The collection would fit nicely into the Brandywine's mission and its existing collections. And Jim Duff, the Director, and his staff would know how to use it with imagination.

So we discussed individually with each of our four children the proposal to bequeath the bulk of the collection of all our Pyle items to the Brandywine Conservancy. The children were the ones who would ultimately sustain the loss. Without exception they all agreed to our plan. We talked with Frolic and Jim Duff and they were enthusiastic. We put the plan into action.

Checklist of the Exhibition

OIL PAINTINGS

1. ***The Master Caused Us to Have Some Beere***, **1883**
   Oil on canvas, 15 x 13 inches (38.1 x 33.0 cm)
   Unsigned
   Illustration for George William Curtis, "Christmas,"
   Harper's New Monthly, December 1883.

2. ***The Wise Fools of Gotham ("To Sea in a Bowl!"***
   Exclaimed the Puzzled Pembroke), **1886**
   Oil on board, 12¾ x 17 1/8 inches (32.4 x 44.0 cm)
   Signed lower right: H. Pyle
   Illustration for Elbridge S. Brooks, "A Cycle of
   Children," *Wide Awake*, April 1886. Also reproduced
   in Elbridge S. Brooks, *Storied Holidays* (Boston:
   D. Lathrop Company, 1887).

3. ***Coureurs De Bois in Town***, **1888**
   Oil on canvas, 20 x 13⅝ inches (50.8 x 14.6 cm)
   Signed lower right: H. Pyle
   Illustration for C. H. Farnham, "Canadian Voyageurs
   on the Saguenay," *Harper's New Monthly*, March 1888.

4. ***The Saving of King Inge***, **1888**
   Oil on canvas on board, 19¾ x 14 inches
   (50.2 x 35.6 cm)
   Signed lower right: H. Pyle
   Illustration for H. H. Boyesen, "Inge, the Boy-King,"
   Wide Awake, December 1888.

(cat. 133) Sketch of a Man with a
Hat, undated

(cat. 9) **The Wreck**, *1892*

(cat. 35) "Quo Vadis, Domine!" 1897

(cat. 70) **Tacy Kelp**, *1879*

5. *He Lay Silent and Still (He Lay Silent and Still with His Face Half Buried in the Sand)*, **1890**
Oil on canvas, 23¼ x 15¼ inches (59.1 x 38.7 cm)
Signed lower right: H Pyle
Illustration for Howard Pyle, "Blueskin, the Pirate," *Northwestern Miller*, December 1890.

6. *On the Way to Tyburn*, **1890**
Oil on canvas on board, 15 x 24⅛ inches
(38.1 x 61.3 cm)
Signed lower left: H. Pyle
Illustration for Howard Pyle, "A Famous Chapbook Villain," *Harper's New Monthly*, July 1890.

7. *Grandmother's Story of Bunker Hill Battle*, **1892**
Oil on canvas, 24 x 16 inches (61.0 x 40.6 cm)
Signed lower left: H. Pyle
Illustration for *Poetical Works of Oliver Wendell Holmes*, vol. 2 (Boston and New York: Houghton, Mifflin, 1892).

8. *The Last Leaf*, **1892**
Oil on canvas, 24¼ x 16⅛ inches (61.6 x 40.9 cm)
Signed lower right: Pyle
Illustration for *Poetical Works of Oliver Wendell Holmes*, vol. 1 (Boston and New York: Houghton, Mifflin, 1892).

9. *The Wreck*, **1892**
Oil on canvas, 24¼ x 36⅜ inches (61.6 x 92.4 cm)
Signed lower right: H. Pyle
Illustration for Howard Pyle, "Among the Sand Hills," *Harper's New Monthly*, September 1892.

10. *Along the Canal in Old Manhattan*, **1893**

    Oil on board, 18½ x 11⅞ inches (47.0 x 30.2 cm)

    Signed lower right: Pyle

    Illustration for Thomas A. Janvier, "The Evolution of
    New York," *Harper's New Monthly*, May 1893. Also
    reproduced Thomas A. Janvier, *In Old New York*
    (New York: Harper & Brothers, 1894).

11. *The Death of Braddock*, **1893**

    Oil on board, 18¼ x 11⅞ inches (46.4 x 30.2 cm)

    Signed upper left: H. Pyle 93

    Illustration for Henry C. Pickering, "An
    Unpublished Autograph Narrative by Washington,"
    Scribner's, May 1893. Also reproduced in Philip G.
    Hamerton, *The Art of the American Wood Engraver*
    (New York: Charles Scribner's Sons, 1894); and
    E. Benjamin Andrews, *History of the United States*
    (New York: Charles Scribner's Sons, 1895).

12. *A Night in the Village Street*, **1893**

    Oil on canvas, 24¾ x 17⅞ inches (62.9 x 45.4 cm)

    Signed lower left: Pyle

    Illustration for Howard Pyle, "A Soldier of Fortune,"
    Harper's New Monthly, December 1893.

13. *He Had Found the Captain Agreeable and
    Companionable*, **1894**

    Oil on board, 16 x 10⅝ inches (40.6 x 27.0 cm)

    Signed upper right: H. Pyle

    Illustration for Thomas A. Janvier, "The Sea-Robbers
    of New York," *Harper's New Monthly*, November 1894.

(cat. 72) **Cor Cordia: A Christmas
Greeting from Thy Husband**, *1881*

(cat. 39) ***The Charge***, 1904

(cat. 37) **Connecticut Settlers Entering the Western Reserve**, *1902*

(cat. 75) **The Sea-Gull's Song**, 1882

14. *A Reminiscence of the Marigold*, **1894**
    Oil on board, 12 x 8 inches (30.5 x 20.3 cm)
    Signed lower right: H. Pyle
    Illustration for Oliver Wendell Holmes, *The Autocrat
    of the Breakfast-Table* (Cambridge: Riverside Press, 1894).

15. *"Speak up, Boy, — Speak up," Said the Gentleman*,
    1894
    Oil on board, 15⅞ x 10⅜ inches (39.7 x 26.4 cm)
    Signed lower right: H.P.
    Illustration for Howard Pyle, "Jack Ballister's
    Fortunes," *St. Nicholas*, July 1894. Also reproduced
    in Howard Pyle, *Jack Ballister's Fortunes* (New York:
    Century Company, 1895).

16. *The Trotting Match*, **1894**
    Oil on board, 12 x 8 inches (30.5 x 20.3 cm)
    Signed lower right: H. Pyle
    Illustration for Oliver Wendell Holmes, *The Autocrat
    of the Breakfast-Table* (Cambridge: Riverside Press, 1894).

17. *The Admiral Came in His Gig of State*, **1895**
Oil on board, 19¾ x 14 inches (50.2 x 35.6 cm)
Signed lower right: Pyle
Illustration for James Jeffrey Roche, "A Business Transaction," *Century*, June 1895.

18. *The **Constitution's** Last Fight*, **1895**
Oil on board, 16¼ x 10 inches (41.2 x 25.4 cm)
Unsigned
Illustration for James Jeffrey Roche, "The Constitution's Last Fight," *Century*, September 1895. Also reproduced in Ernest Ingersoll, *The Book of the Ocean* (New York: Century Company, 1898).

19. *The Pirates Fire upon the Fugitives*, **1895**
Oil on board, 16 x 10 inches (40.6 x 25.4 cm)
Signed lower right: H. Pyle
Illustration for Howard Pyle, "Jack Ballister's Fortunes," *St. Nicholas*, April 1895. Also reproduced in Howard Pyle, *Jack Ballister's Fortunes* (New York: Century Company, 1895).

20. *She is Drunk. It Will Soon Pass Away (Some of the By-Standers Said: "She is Drunk. It Will Soon Pass Away")*, **1895**
Oil on board, 16 x 10½ inches (40.6 x 26.7 cm)
Signed lower right: H.P.
Illustration for Thomas A. Janvier, "New York Slave Traders," *Harper's New Monthly*, January 1895.

21. *The Surrender of Captain Pearson (The Surrender of Captain Pearson on the Deck of the **Bon Homme Richard**)*, **1895**
Oil on board, 18 x 11¾ inches (45.7 x 29.8 cm)
Signed lower right: H.P.
Illustration for Molly E. Seawell, "Paul Jones," *Century*, April 1895.

22. *We Escaped in the Boat*, **1895**
Oil on board, 16 x 10¼ inches (40.6 x 26.0 cm)
Signed lower right: H.P.
Illustration for Thomas A. Janvier, "New York Slave Traders," *Harper's New Monthly*, January 1895.

23. *The Champlain Tows*, **1896**
Oil on board, 11 x 12¼ inches (27.9 x 31.1 cm)
Unsigned
Illustration for Howard Pyle, "Through Inland Waters," part 2, *Harper's New Monthly*, June 1896.

24. *The Convalescent*, **1896**
Oil on board, 7¼ x 7¼ inches (18.4 x 18.4 cm)
Unsigned
Illustration for Howard Pyle, "The Romance of an Ambrotype," *Harper's New Monthly*, December 1896.

25. *Floating Neighbors*, **1896**
Oil on board, 12⅛ x 10⅛ inches (30.8 x 25.7 cm)
Signed mid-left: P
Illustration for Howard Pyle, "Through Inland Waters," part 1, *Harper's New Monthly*, May 1896.

(cat. 36) ***A Dream of Young Summer,*** *1901*

(cat. 38) **Roger Bacon**, *1903*

26. *The Floating Water Home*, **1896**
Oil on board, 8¼ x 6½ inches (21.0 x 16.5 cm)
Signed lower right: P
Illustration for Howard Pyle, "Through Inland
Waters," part 1, *Harper's New Monthly*, May 1896.

27. Headpiece for *The Romance of an Ambrotype*, **1896**
Oil on board, 7¾ x 11½ inches (19.7 x 29.2 cm)
Signed center right: H. P.
Illustration for Howard Pyle, "The Romance of an
Ambrotype," *Harper's New Monthly*, December 1896.

28. *Leisurely Drifting through Farm Lands*, **1896**
Oil on board, 7⅛ x 12⅝ inches (18.1 x 32.1 cm)
Unsigned
Illustration for Howard Pyle, "Through Inland
Waters," part 1, *Harper's New Monthly*, May 1896.

29. Tailpiece for *The Romance of an Ambrotype*, **1896**
Oil on board, 4 x 6 inches (10.2 x 15.2 cm)
Signed lower left: H. P.
Illustration for Howard Pyle, "The Romance of an
Ambrotype," *Harper's New Monthly*, December 1896.

30. *These Little Gardens*, **1896**
Oil on board, 6½ x 6⅞ inches (16.5 x 17.5 cm)
Signed lower left: P
Illustration for Howard Pyle, "Through Inland
Waters," part 1, *Harper's New Monthly*, May 1896.

31. *Vignette* (woman on a houseboat), **1896**
Oil on board, 7½ x 9½ inches (19.1 x 24.1 cm)
Signed lower right: P

Unpublished illustration for Howard Pyle, "Through
Inland Waters," part 2, *Harper's New Monthly*, June
1896.

32. *Wide Damp Reaches of Brightness*, **1896**
Oil on board, 4 x 10¾ inches (10.2 x 27.3 cm)
Unsigned
Illustration for Howard Pyle, "Through Inland
Waters," part 1, *Harper's New Monthly*, May 1896.

33. *The Mizzentop of the* **Redoubtable**, **1897**
Oil on canvas, 28 x 18¼ inches (71.1 x 46.4 cm)
Signed lower right: H. Pyle
Illustration for A.T. Mahan, "Nelson at Trafalgar,"
Century, March 1897.

34. *Nelson At the Battle of Copenhagen (Nelson Sealing
the Letter to the Crown Prince of Denmark at the
Battle of Copenhagen)*, **1897**
Oil on canvas, 16⅛ x 25⅛ inches (40.9 x 63.8 cm)
Signed lower right: Pyle
Illustration for A.T. Mahan, "The Battle of
Copenhagen," *Century*, February 1897. Also repro-
duced in Howard Pyle, *Catalogue of Drawings
Illustrating the Life of General Washington, and of
Colonial Life* (Boston: St. Botolph Club, 1897).

35. *"Quo Vadis, Domine!"* **1897**
Oil on canvas, 25⅞ x 16⅞ inches (65.7 x 42.9 cm)
Signed lower right: H. Pyle
Illustration for Henryk Sienkiewicz, *Quo Vadis*,
Jeremiah Curtin, trans. (Boston: Little Brown, 1897).

36. *A Dream of Young Summer*, **1901**

Oil on canvas, 22⅛ x 12⅛ inches (56.2 x 30.8 cm)

Signed lower right: H. Pyle

Inscribed lower left: To Augustus Saint Gaudens this Picture of Young Summer with the Fraternal Greeting of His Brother in Art.

Illustration for Edith M. Thomas, "A Dream of Young Summer," *Harper's Monthly*, June 1901.

37. *Connecticut Settlers Entering the Western Reserve*, **1902**

Oil on board, 16⅛ x 24 inches (40.9 x 61.0 cm)

Signed lower right: Pyle

Illustration for Alfred Mathews, "A Story of Three States," *Scribner's*, May 1902.

Also reproduced in Wilbur F. Gordy, *A History of the United States* (New York: Charles Scribner's Sons, 1904)

38. *Roger Bacon*, **1903**

Oil on canvas, 35⅛ x 20⅛ inches (89.2 x 5.1 cm)

Signed lower right: H. Pyle

Frontispiece for Thomas Frognall Dibdin, *The Bibliomania; or, Book Madness*, vol. 2 (Boston: Bibliophile Society, 1903). Also reproduced in W.H.W. Bicknell, *Portfolio of Etchings* (Bibliophile Society, Boston, 1903).

39. *The Charge*, **1904**

Oil on canvas, 24⅛ x 16⅛ inches (61.3 x 40.9 cm)

Signed lower left: H. Pyle

Illustration for Robert W. Chambers, "Non-Combatants," *Harper's Monthly*, November 1904.

(cat. 99) Drawing for Grolier Club bookplate, ca. 1890

(cat. 40) Frontispiece for **The Eclogues of Vergil**, *1904*

40. Frontispiece for *The Eclogues of Vergil*, **1904**
Oil on board, 18½ x 11⅛ inches (47 x 28.2 cm)
Signed mid-right: H. Pyle
Illustration for Publius Vergilius Maro, *The Eclogues of Vergil*, Baron Bowen, trans. (Boston: Privately printed by Nathan Haskell Dole, 1904).

41. *The Haunted House (Catherine Duke Quickened her Steps)*, **1904**
Oil on canvas, 24¾ x 16 inches (62.9 x 40.6 cm)
Inscribed at bottom: "The Haunted House" to Cass Gilbert from Howard Pyle 1907
Illustration for Mary E. Wilkins Freeman, "The Gold," *Harper's Monthly*, December 1904.

42. *The Doge Sat Alone in a Great Carven Chair*, **1905**
Oil on canvas, 25 x 16 inches (63.5 x 40.6 cm)
Signed lower left: Pyle
Illustration for Justus Miles Foreman, "The Island of Enchantment," *Harper's Monthly*, September 1905. Also reproduced in Justus Miles Foreman, *The Island of Enchantment* (New York: Harper & Brothers, 1905).

43. *Henry V at Agincourt (He Came to Her — In His Helmet a Fox Brush Spangled with Jewels)*, **1905**
Oil on canvas, 24¼ x 16¼ inches (61.6 x 41.2 cm)
Signed lower right: Pyle
Illustration for James Branch Cabell, "The Fox Brush," *Harper's Monthly*, August 1905.

44. *The Spy (She Drew Bridle Listening — There Was No Sound)*, **1905**
Oil on canvas, 24⅛ x 16¼ inches (61.3 x 41.2 cm)
Unsigned
Illustration for Robert W. Chambers, "Special Messenger," *Harper's Monthly*, February 1905.

45. *The Lighters Were Soon Alongside*, **1907**
Oil on board, 12¼ x 9½ inches (31.1 x 24.1 cm)
Signed lower right: P
Illustration for Thomas V. Briggs, "The Cruise of the Caribee," *Harper's Monthly*, December 1907.

46. *The Man with the Broken Nose*, **1907**
Oil on board, 10 x 8¼ inches (25.4 x 21.0 cm)
Inscribed lower right: To Dr. Joseph Lasinsky from Howard Pyle
Illustration for Howard Pyle, "The Ruby of Kishmoor," *Harper's Monthly*, August 1907. Also reproduced in Howard Pyle, *The Ruby of Kishmoor* (New York: Harper & Brothers, 1908).

47. *The Negress Beckoned Him to Draw Nearer*, **1907**
Oil on board, 11½ x 5 inches (29.2 x 12.7 cm)
Signed lower right: Pyle
Inscribed: To J.E. G. From H.P. 1907
Illustration for Howard Pyle, "The Ruby of Kishmoor," *Harper's Monthly*, August 1907. Also reproduced in Howard Pyle, *The Ruby of Kishmoor* (New York: Harper & Brothers, 1908).

48. *The Rest Were Shot and Thrown Overboard*, **1907**
Oil on board, 9⅛ x 12⅛ inches (23.2 x 30.8 cm)
Signed lower right: P
Illustration for Thomas V. Briggs, "The Cruise of the Caribee," *Harper's Monthly*, December 1907.

(cat. 41) **The Haunted House (Catherine Duke Quickened her Steps)**, 1904

114

(cat. 42) **The Doge Sat Alone in a Great Carven Chair**, *1905*

49. **'Tween Decks of the Slaver**, **1907**
Oil on board, 12¼ x 9¼ inches (31.1 x 23.5 cm)
Signed lower left: P
Illustration for Thomas V. Briggs, "The Cruise of the Caribee," *Harper's Monthly*, December 1907.

50. Illustrative border for **Edric and Sylvaine** (left-hand page), **1908**
Oil on board, 13½ x 8½ inches (34.3 x 21.6 cm)
Unsigned
Illustration for Brian Hooker, "Edric and Sylvaine," *Harper's Monthly*, August 1908.

51. Illustrative border for **Edric and Sylvaine** (right-hand page), **1908**
Oil on board, 14 x 18 inches (35.6 x 45.7 cm)
Unsigned
Illustration for Brian Hooker, "Edric and Sylvaine," *Harper's Monthly*, August 1908.

52. **The Passing of Doña Victoria**, **1908**
Oil on canvas, 32¼ x 21⅜ inches (81.9 x 54.3 cm)
Signed lower right: Pyle
Illustration for Perceval Gibbon, "Doña Victoria," *Harper's Monthly*, February 1908.

53. **The Shell**, **1908**
Oil on canvas, 30¼ x 20 inches (76.8 x 50.8 cm)
Signed lower right: H. Pyle
Illustration for William W. Lord, Jr., "A Child at the Siege of Vicksburg," *Harper's Monthly*, December 1908.

54. **Then the Real Fight Began**, **1908**
Oil on canvas, 30¼ x 20⅛ inches (76.8 x 51.1 cm)
Signed lower right: H. Pyle
Illustration for Hampton L. Carson, "Pennsylvania's Defiance of the United States," *Harper's Monthly*, October 1908.

55. Title page for **The Mysterious Chest**, **1908**
Oil on board, 24 x 18 inches (61.0 x 45.7 cm)
Unsigned
Illustration for Howard Pyle, "The Mysterious Chest," *Harper's Monthly*, December 1908.

56. Marginal illustration for **The Salem Wolf**, **1909**
Oil on board, 11⅜ x 10⅛ inches (28.9 x 25.7 cm)
Unsigned
Illustration for Howard Pyle, "The Salem Wolf," *Harper's Monthly*, December 1909.

57. Marginal illustration for **The Salem Wolf**, **1909**
Oil on board, 3⅜ x 5¼ inches (8.6 x 13.3 cm)
Unsigned
Illustration for Howard Pyle, "The Salem Wolf," *Harper's Monthly*, December 1909.

58. Marginal illustration for **The Salem Wolf**, **1909**
Oil on board, 5¼ x 4⅝ inches (13.3 x 11.8 cm)
Unsigned
Illustration for Howard Pyle, "The Salem Wolf," *Harper's Monthly*, December 1909.

59. *She Saw Herself for What He Had Said, and Swooned*, **1909**
Oil on canvas, 27⅛ x 18⅛ inches (68.9 x 46.1 cm)
Signed lower right: Pyle
Illustration for Josephine Daskam Bacon, "The Castle on the Dunes," *Harper's Monthly*, September 1909.

60. Title page for *The Salem Wolf*, **1909**
Oil on board, 24½ x 16 inches (62.2 x 16 cm)
Signed lower corner: P
Illustration for Howard Pyle, "The Salem Wolf," *Harper's Monthly*, December 1909.

61. *Vitia and the Governor*, **1909**
Oil on canvas, 24¼ x 16¼ inches (61.6 x 41.2 cm)
Signed lower right: H. Pyle
Illustration for Justus Miles Forman, "The Garden of Eden," *Harper's Monthly*, May 1909.

62. *The Wolf and Dr. Wilkinson (Once it Chased Doctor Wilkinson Into the Very Town Itself)*, **1909**
Oil on canvas, 27⅞ x 18⅛ inches (70.8 x 46.1 cm)
Signed lower left: Pyle
Illustration for Howard Pyle, "The Salem Wolf," *Harper's Monthly*, December 1909.

63. Illustrative border for *Ysobel de Corveaux* (left-hand page), **1910**
Oil on board, 12 x 9½ inches (30.5 x 24.1 cm)
Unsigned
Illustration for Brian Hooker, "Ysobel de Corveaux," *Harper's Monthly*, August 1910.

64. Illustrative border for *Ysobel de Corveaux* (right-hand page), **1910**
Oil on board, 9⅝ x 14¾ inches (24.5 x 37.4 cm)
Unsigned
Illustration for Brian Hooker, "Ysobel de Corveaux," *Harper's Monthly*, August 1910.

65. *The Prisoner*, **1910**
Oil on board, 15¾ x 3⅞ inches (40 x 9.9 cm)
Unsigned
Illustration for Brian Hooker, "Ysobel de Corveaux," *Harper's Monthly*, August 1910.

66. Painting for Howard Pyle bookplate, undated
Oil on wood panel, 12 x 7⅛ inches (30.5 x 18.1 cm)
Inscribed at bottom: Ex Libris Howard Pyle

67. Head of a Woman, undated
Oil on board, 5⅞ x 11 inches (14.9 x 27.9 cm)
Unsigned

68. *Ye Queen of Hearts*, undated
Oil on wood box, 6⅞ x 3 inches (17.5 x 7.6 cm)
Unsigned
Painted for Frank Schoonover

(cat. 43) Henry V at Agincourt (He Came to Her — In His Helmet a Fox Brush Spangled with Jewels), 1905

118

(cat. 44) *The Spy (She Drew Bridle Listening — There Was No Sound)*, 1905

(cat. 134) ***A View in Jamaica****,*
undated

WATERCOLORS AND DRAWINGS

69. ***The Little Boys Cheered Vigorously (The Little Boys
Cheered Vigorously as He Pushed Off)****,* **1879**
Ink on paper, 11¾ x 8¾ inches (29.8 x 22.2 cm)
Signed lower right: HP
Illustration for Howard Pyle, "The Last Revel in
Printz Hall," *Harper's New Monthly*, September 1879.

70. ***Tacy Kelp****,* **1879**
Ink on paper, 9 x 5¾ inches (2.9 x 14.6 cm)
Signed lower right: P
Illustration for Howard Pyle, "The Last Revel in
Printz Hall," *Harper's New Monthly*, September 1879.

71. ***Woman at a Spinning Wheel****,* **1879**
Watercolor on paper, 11½ x 8¾ inches (29.2 x 22.2 cm)
Signed lower left: HPyle/'79

72. ***Cor Cordia: A Christmas Greeting from Thy
Husband****,* **1881**
Watercolor on vellum, 10½ x 6⅝ inches (26.7 x 16.8 cm)
Inscribed lower right, "MDCCCLXXXI †MASS"

73. Study for ***Suspicious Strangers****,* **1881**
Pencil on paper, 4⅞ x 8⅛ inches (12.4 x 20.7 cm)
Unsigned

74. ***Suspicious Strangers****,* **1881**
Watercolor on paper stretched on canvas, 20 x 30
inches (50.8 x 76.2 cm)
Signed and inscribed lower right, "Suspicious
Strangers/Howard Pyle.pinxt/Jan.1881"

75. *The Sea-Gull's Song*, **1882**

Watercolor on paper, 11¼ x 7⅛ inches (28.6 x 18.1 cm)

Signed lower right: Howard Pyle

Illustration for Howard Pyle, "The Sea-Gull's Song," *Harper's Weekly*, November 25, 1882.

76. *Endicott Cutting the Cross Out of the English Flag*, **1883**

Gouache on paper, 15¾ x 13¼ inches (40.0 x 33.7 cm)

Signed lower right: HPyle

Illustration for Thomas Wentworth Higginson, "An English Nation," *Harper's New Monthly*, April 1883. Also reproduced in *Harper's Encyclopedia of United States History*, vol. 6 (New York: Harper & Brothers, 1902).

77. *A Verse with a Moral but No Name*, **1884**

Ink on paper, 16 x 11 inches (40.6 x 27.9 cm)

Signed lower right: H Pyle

Illustration for Howard Pyle, "A Verse with a Moral but No Name," *Harper's Young People*, March 11, 1884. Also reproduced in Howard Pyle, *Pepper and Salt; or, Seasoning for Young Folk* (New York: Harper & Brothers, 1886).

78. *Ye Song of ye Gossips*, **1884**

Page with title, illustration and verse

Ink on paper, 13¼ x 9½ inches (33.7 x 24.1 cm)

Signed lower right: H. Pyle

Illustration for Howard Pyle, "Ye Song of ye Gossips," *Harper's Young People*, August 5, 1884. Also reproduced in Howard Pyle, *Pepper and Salt; or, Seasoning for Young Folk* (New York: Harper & Brothers, 1886).

79. Headpiece for *How One Turned his Trouble to some account*, **1885**

Ink on paper, 2⅞ x 8 inches (7.3 x 20.3 cm)

Signed lower center: HP

Illustration for Howard Pyle, "How One Turned His Trouble to Some Account," *Harper's Young People*, November 10, 1885. Also reproduced in Howard Pyle, *The Wonder Clock; or, Four and Twenty Marvelous Titles, Being One for Each Hour of the Day* (New York: Harper & Brothers, 1888).

80. *The Brave Soldier bringeth his Trouble to ye town along with him*, **1885**

Ink on paper, 9⅝ x 6⅝ inches (24.5 x 16.8 cm)

Signed lower right: HP

Illustration for Howard Pyle, "How One Turned His Trouble to Some Account," *Harper's Young People*, November 10, 1885. Also reproduced in Howard Pyle, *The Wonder Clock; or, Four and Twenty Marvelous Titles, Being One for Each Hour of the Day* (New York: Harper & Brothers, 1888).

81. *Here the Brave Soldier brings his trouble before the king to find if it shall follow him wherever he goes*, **1885**

Ink on paper, 9½ x 6½ inches (24.1 x 16.5 cm)

Signed lower right: HP

Illustration for Howard Pyle, "How One Turned His Trouble to Some Account," *Harper's Young People*, November 10, 1885. Also reproduced in Howard Pyle, *The Wonder Clock; or, Four and Twenty Marvelous Titles, Being One for Each Hour of the Day* (New York: Harper & Brothers, 1888).

(cat. 46) **The Man with the Broken Nose**, *1907*

(cat. 47) **The Negress Beckoned Him to
Draw Nearer**, *1907*

82. *Half-title for **Pepper and Salt**,* **1886**
Ink on paper, 5½ x 4 inches (14.0 x 10.2cm)
Signed lower center: H.P.
Illustration for Howard Pyle, *Pepper and Salt; or, Seasoning for Young Folk* (New York: Harper & Brothers, 1886).

83. Headpiece for ***Pepper and Salt*** , **1886**
Ink on paper, 2 x 6¾ inches (5.1 x 17.1 cm)
Signed lower right: H.P.
Illustration for Howard Pyle, *Pepper and Salt; or, Seasoning for Young Folk* (New York: Harper & Brothers, 1886).

84. Tailpiece for ***Pepper and Salt*** (List of Illustrations), **1886**
Ink on paper, 3¼ x 5¾ inches (8.3 x 14.6 cm)
Signed at center: H.P.
Illustration for Howard Pyle, *Pepper and Salt; or, Seasoning for Young Folk* (New York: Harper & Brothers, 1886).

85. Tailpiece for ***Pepper and Salt*** (Preface), **1886**
Ink on paper, 3⅛ x 4¾ inches (8.0 x 12.1)
Signed at center: H.P.
Illustration for Howard Pyle, *Pepper and Salt; or, Seasoning for Young Folk* (New York: Harper & Brothers, 1886).

86. *Apollo Slaying the Python*, **1887**
Watercolor on paper, 11¼ x 8¾ inches (28.6 x 22.2 cm)
Signed lower left: H. Pyle
Illustration for James Baldwin, *A Story of the Golden Age* (New York: Charles Scribner's Sons, 1887).

87. *I am Captain John Mackra ("I am Captain John Mackra," Said I, and I Sat Down upon the Gunwale of the Boat)*, **1887**
Watercolor on paper, 10 x 15⅝ inches (25.4 x 39.7 cm)
Signed lower right: H. Pyle
Illustration for Howard Pyle, "The Rose of Paradise," *Harper's Weekly*, July 9, 1887. Also reproduced in Howard Pyle, *Rose of Paradise* (New York: Harper & Brothers, 1888).

88. *I Rose Slowly from My Chair (I Rose Slowly from My Chair, and Stood with My Hand Leaning upon the Table)*, **1887**
Watercolor on paper, 10 x 15 inches (24.5 x 38.1 cm)
Signed lower left: H. Pyle
Illustration for Howard Pyle, "The Rose of Paradise," *Harper's Weekly*, July 9, 1887. Also reproduced in Howard Pyle, *Rose of Paradise* (New York: Harper & Brothers, 1888).

89. *Palamedes Tests the Madness of Odysseus*, **1887**
Watercolor on paper, 9¾ x 12¾ inches (24.8 x 32.4 cm)
Signed lower right: H.Pyle
Illustration for James Baldwin, *A Story of the Golden Age* (New York: Charles Scribner's Sons, 1887).

90. *The Prince Pours Water into the Barrel*, **1888**
Ink on paper, 7⅛ x 6⅝ inches (18.1 x 16.8 cm)
Signed at center right: HP
Illustration for Howard Pyle, "The Princess on the Glass Hill," *Harper's Young People*, July 24, 1888.

91. *The Two Thieves*, **1889**

Ink on paper, 5⅜ x 9¾ inches (13.7 x 24.8 cm)

Unsigned

Illustration for Howard Pyle, "Wisdom's Wages and Folly's Pay," *Harper's Young People*, November 5, 1889. Also reproduced in Howard Pyle, *Twilight Land* (New York: Harper & Brothers, 1895).

92. *Decorative Initial I*, **1890**

Watercolor on paper, 7¼ x 2½ inches (18.4 x 6.4 cm)

Unsigned

Illustration for Howard Pyle, "Jamaica, New and Old," part 1, *Harper's New Monthly*, January 1890.

93. *Executing an Intricate Passage*, **1890**

Ink on paper, 12⅝ x 9⅝ inches (32.1. x 24.5 cm)

Signed lower right: P

Illustration for James Lane Allen, "Flute and Violin," *Harper's New Monthly*, December 1890. Also reproduced in James Lane Allen, *Flute and Violin and Other Kentucky Tales and Romances* (New York: Harper & Brothers, 1891).

94. *Gallows Point*, **1890**

Watercolor on paper, 7⅝ x 4½ inches (19.4 x 11.4 cm)

Signed lower left: P

Illustration for Howard Pyle, "Jamaica, New and Old," part 1, *Harper's New Monthly*, January 1890.

95. *He Met a Poor Woman Coming Home from the Market*, **1890**

Ink on paper, 14½ x 12½ inches (36.8 x 31.8 cm)

Signed lower right: P

Illustration for Howard Pyle, "Much Shall Have More and Little Shall Have Less," *Harper's Young People*, November 4, 1890. Also reproduced in Howard Pyle, *Twilight Land* (New York: Harper & Brothers, 1895).

96. *It Was a Very Gay Dinner*, **1890**

Ink on paper, 6½ x 9½ inches (16.5 x 24.1 cm)

Signed lower right: P

Illustration for James Lane Allen, "Flute and Violin," *Harper's New Monthly*, December 1890. Also reproduced in James Lane Allen, *Flute and Violin and Other Kentucky Tales and Romances* (New York: Harper & Brothers, 1891).

97. *The King and the Beggar Feasted*, **1890**

Ink on paper, 15 x 12 inches (38.1 x 30.5 cm)

Signed lower left: P

Illustration for Howard Pyle, "All Things Are as Fate Wills," *Harper's Young People*, October 14, 1890. Also reproduced in Howard Pyle, *Twilight Land* (New York: Harper & Brothers, 1895).

98. *Village Scene in Jamaica*, **1890**

Watercolor on paper, 6 x 11 inches (15.2 x 27.9 cm)

Signed lower right: HP

Illustration for Howard Pyle, "Jamaica, New and Old," part 2, *Harper's New Monthly*, February 1890.

99. Drawing for Grolier Club Bookplate, ca. 1890
Ink on paper, 5¼ x 4⅛ inches (13.3 x 10.5 cm)
Signed lower right: H.P.

100. *Along the Highway Furiously*, **1891**
Ink on paper, 5⅞ x 4⅞ inches (14.7 x 12.4 cm)
Signed lower right: P
Illustration for Louise Imogen Guiney, "Peter Rugg:
Ye Bostonian," *Scribner's*, December, 1891.

101. Alternate tailpiece for *Peter Rugg Ye Bostonian*, **1891**
Ink on paper, 7¾ x 4⅞ inches (19.7 x 12.4 cm)
Signed lower right: Pyle
Unpublished illustration for Louise Imogen Guiney,
"Peter Rugg Ye Bostonian," *Scribner's*, December,
1891.

102. *He Called the Wisest Men of the Island to Him*, **1891**
Ink on paper, 15 x 12 inches (38.1 x 30.5 cm)
Signed lower right: P
Illustration for Howard Pyle, "The Enchanted
Island," *Harper's Young People*, December 22, 1891.
Also reproduced in Howard Pyle, *Twilight Land*
(New York: Harper & Brothers, 1895).

103. *He Came to the Cross-roads and the Stone Cross*,
1891
Ink on paper, 8⅝ x 6⅞ inches (21.9 x 17.5 cm)
Signed lower right: P
Illustration for Howard Pyle, "The Fruit of
Happiness," *Harper's Young People*, January 13, 1891.
Also reproduced in Howard Pyle, *Twilight Land*
(New York: Harper & Brothers, 1895).

104. Title page for *The Enchanted Island*, **1891**
Ink on paper, 15 x 12 inches (38.1 x 30.5 cm)
Signed lower right: HP
Illustration for Howard Pyle, "The Enchanted
Island," parts 1 & 2, *Harper's Young People*, December
15 and 22, 1891. Also reproduced in Howard Pyle,
Twilight Land (New York: Harper & Brothers, 1895).

105. *The Deacon's Masterpiece; or, the Wonderful
"One-Hoss-Shay,"* **1892**
Watercolor on paper, 5 x 6⅝ inches (12.7 x 16.8 cm)
Signed lower left: HP
Unpublished version

106. Decorative border for *Dorothy Q*, **1892**
Ink on paper, 10⅜ x 6⅞ inches (26.4 x 17.5 cm)
Unsigned
Illustrated in Oliver Wendell Holmes's, *Dorothy Q,
Together with A Ballad of the Boston Tea Party and
Grandmother's Story of Bunker Hill Battle* (Boston and
New York: Houghton, Mifflin, 1893).

107. *The Demon Leaped from the Earth*, **1892**
Ink on paper, 14½ x 9⅛ inches (36.8 x 23.2 cm)
Signed lower right: P
Illustration for Howard Pyle, "The Talisman of
Solomon," part 1, *Harper's Young People*, March 29,
1892. Also reproduced in Howard Pyle, *Twilight
Land* (New York: Harper & Brothers, 1895).

(cat. 53) ***The Shell***, *1908*

126

(cat. 54) **Then the Real Fight Began,** *1908*

108. *"I Think Everybody Has Gone Mad," Said the Young Man*, **1892**

Ink on paper, 14½ x 9⅛ inches (36.8 x 23.2 cm)

Signed lower right: P

Illustration for Howard Pyle, "The Talisman of Solomon," part 2, *Harper's Young People*, April 5, 1892.

109. *Prescott on the Rampart*, **1893**

Ink on paper, 6⅝ x 4⅜ inches (16.8 x 11.2 cm)

Signed lower right: P

Illustration for Oliver Wendell Holmes, *Dorothy Q, Together with A Ballad of the Boston Tea Party, and Grandmother's Story of Bunker Hill Battle* (Cambridge: Riverside Press, 1893).

110. *They are Baffled, Not Defeated*, **1893**

Ink on paper, 8 x 5¼ inches (20.3 x 13.3 cm)

Signed lower right: P

Inscribed: To S.M. Palmer from/his teacher <u>Howard Pyle</u>/Wilmington [illeg.] 17th 1900.

Illustration for Oliver Wendell Holmes, *Dorothy Q, Together with A Ballad of the Boston Tea Party and Grandmother's Story of Bunker Hill Battle* (Cambridge; Riverside Press, 1893). Also reproduced in Oliver Wendell Holmes, *Grandmother's Story of Bunker Hill Battle as She Saw It from the Belfry* (Boston and New York: Houghton, Mifflin, 1903).

111. Title page for *A Ballad of the Boston Tea-Party*, **1893**

Ink on paper, 10⅛ x 7 inches (25.7 x 17.8 cm)

Unsigned

Illustration for Oliver Wendell Holmes, *Dorothy Q, Together with A Ballad of the Boston Tea Party and Grandmother's Story of Bunker Hill Battle* (Cambridge: Riverside Press, 1893).

112. *Melancholia*, **1895**

Ink on paper, 10 x 15¼ inches (25.4 x 38.7 cm)

Signed lower right: HP

Illustration for W.D. Howells, *Impression: Stops of Various Quills* (New York: Harper & Brothers, 1895).

113. *Untitled* (angel playing a flute), **1895**

Ink on paper, 3¼ x 5½ inches (8.3 x 14.0 cm)

Signed lower right: HP / Howard Pyle

Illustration for W.D. Howells, *Impression: Stops of Various Quills* (New York: Harper & Brothers, 1895).

114. *'Tis Enough to Make Both Rich Men*, **1896**

Ink on paper, 8⅜ x 6⅜ inches (21.3 x 16.2 cm)

Signed lower right: P

Illustration for Howard Pyle, "Tom Chist and the Treasure Box," *Harper's Round Table*, March 24, 1896. Also reproduced in Howard Pyle, *Stolen Treasures* (New York: Harper & Brothers, 1907).

115. Headpiece for *Fay Song*, **1900**
Ink on paper, 3 x 7⅝ inches (7.6 x 19.4 cm)
Signed lower right: Howard Pyle
Illustration for Edwin Markham, *The Man with the Hoe and Other Poems* (New York: Doubleday and McClure Company, 1900).

116. *The Old Man*, **1902**
Wash on paper, 6½ x 4½ inches (16.5 x 11.4 cm)
Unsigned
Painted by Howard Pyle at 1305 Franklin street as an example to follow by Frank E. Schoonover in illustrating "Fools Gold," *Everybody Magazine*, February 1902.
Unpublished

117. *Excalibur the Sword*, **1903**
Ink on paper, 9⅞ x 6⅛ inches (25.1 x 15.6 cm)
Signed lower right: HP
Inscribed lower right: Copyright 1902/by The Century Co.
Illustration for Howard Pyle, "The Story of King Arthur and His Knights," *St. Nicholas*, March 1903.
Also reproduced in Howard Pyle, *The Story of King Arthur and His Knights* (New York: Charles Scribner's Sons, 1903).

118. *In the Valley of Delight*, **1903**
Ink on paper, 9⅞ x 6⅛ inches (25.1 x 15.6 cm)
Signed lower right: HP
Inscribed lower right: Copyright 1903 by The Century Co.

Illustration for Howard Pyle, "The Story of King Arthur and His Knights," *St. Nicholas*, March 1903.
Also reproduced in Howard Pyle, *The Story of King Arthur and His Knights* (New York: Charles Scribner's Sons, 1903).

119. *The Lady Yvette the Fair*, **1903**
Ink on paper, 9¼ x 6⅞ inches (23.5 x 17.4 cm)
Unsigned
Illustration for Howard Pyle, "The Story of King Arthur and His Knights," *St. Nicholas*, March 1903.

120. *Sea Battle between Two Frigates*, **1903**
Ink on paper, 9¼ x 11⅝ inches (23.5 x 30.0 cm)
Inscribed upper right: To A.E. Becher. From H. Pyle. March 17ᵗʰ / 1903
Created as a prize for the best drawing among competing members of the Sketch Club.

121. *The White Champion meets two Knights at the Mill*, **1903**
Ink on paper, 9⅞ x 6¾ inches (25.1 x 17.1 cm)
Signed lower left: HP
Inscribed at bottom: Copyright 1903 by The Century Company
Illustration for Howard Pyle, "The Story of King Arthur and His Knights," *St. Nicholas*, March 1903.
Also reproduced in Howard Pyle, *The Story of King Arthur and His Knights* (New York: Charles Scribner's Sons, 1903).

*(cat. 55) Title page for **The Mysterious Chest**, 1908*

(cat. 66) Painting for Howard Pyle bookplate, undated

122. *The portrait of a young gentleman who always says "Thank you!"* **1904**
Watercolor on paper, 8⅞ x 3⅞ inches (22.5 x 9.8 cm)
Signed lower right: HP.04
Unpublished

123. *King Mark of Cornwall*, **1905**
Ink on paper, 10 x 7 inches (25.4 x 17.8 cm)
Unsigned
Illustration for Howard Pyle, *The Story of the Champions of the Round Table* (New York: Charles Scribner's Sons, 1905).

124. *Sir Launcelot takes the armor of Sir Kay*, **1905**
Ink on paper, 10 x 7 inches (25.4 x 7.8 cm)
Unsigned
Illustration for Howard Pyle, *The Story of the Champions of the Round Table* (New York: Charles Scribner's Sons, 1905).

125. Tailpiece for *The Story of the Champions of the Round Table*, **1905**
Ink on paper, 7⅜ x 11¼ inches (19.4 x 28.6 cm)
Unsigned
Illustration for Howard Pyle, *The Story of the Champions of the Round Table* (New York: Charles Scribner's Sons, 1905).

126. *The Forest Madman saveth ye Life of King Arthur*, **1907**
Ink on paper, 10 x 7 inches (25.4 x 17.8 cm)
Unsigned
Illustration for Howard Pyle, *The Story of Sir Launcelot and his Companions* (New York: Charles Scribner's Sons, 1907).

127. Placecard for Mrs. Bates, **1908**
Ink on paper, 2¼ x 5⅜ inches (5.8 x 17.8 cm)
Signed lower right: H.P. Oct 22. 1908
Illustration originally for Howard Pyle, *Sir Launcelot and His Companions* (New York: Charles Scribner's Sons, 1907).

128. *The True Spirit of Bridge* (scorecard for studio bridge game), **1908**
Ink on paper, 4⅛ x 3¼ inches (10.5 x 8.3 cm)
Unsigned
Unpublished

129. *The Passing of Sir Gawaine*, **1910**
Ink on paper, 10 x 6⅞ inches (25.4 x 16.8 cm)
Unsigned
Illustration for Howard Pyle, *The Story of the Grail and the Passing of Arthur* (New York: Charles Scribner's Sons, 1910).

130. *Sir Geraint and the Knight of the Sparrow-hawk*, **1910**
Ink on paper, 10 x 7 inches (25.4 x 17.8 cm)
Unsigned
Illustration for Howard Pyle, *The Story of the Grail and the Passing of Arthur* (New York: Charles Scribner's Sons, 1910).

131. *Howard Pyle, His Mark* (sketch of a pirate), undated
Ink on paper, 2⅝ x 5¼ inches (6.7 x 13.3 cm)
Signed at right: Very Sincerely Yours/Howard Pyle/His Mark
Unpublished

132. *The Escape*, undated
Watercolor on paper, 9⅛ x 10 inches (23.3 x 25.5 cm)
Signed lower right: P
Unpublished

133. Sketch of a Man with a Hat, undated
Ink on paper, 5 x 3 inches (12.7 cm x 7.6 cm)
Signed lower right, "HP"
Unpublished

134. *A View in Jamaica*, undated
Watercolor on brown paper, 16¾ x 11½ inches (42.5 x 29.2 cm)
Unsigned
Unpublished

(cat. 61) **Vitia and the Governor**, *1909*

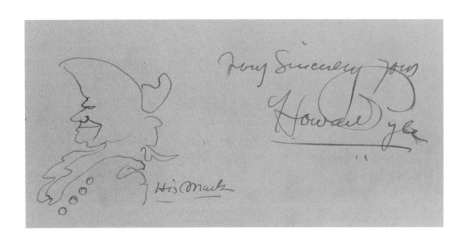

(cat. 131) **Howard Pyle, His Mark** *(sketch of a pirate),*
undated

(cat. 68) **Ye Queen of Hearts**, *undated*

(cat. 127) Placecard for Mrs. Bates, 1908

(cat. 128) **The True Spirit of Bridge**

(scorecard for studio bridge game), 1908